TEACHER'S PET PUBLICATIONS

LITPLAN TEACHER PACK
for
Hatchet
based on the book by
Gary Paulsen

Written by
Barbara M. Linde, MA Ed.

© 1996 Teacher's Pet Publications
All Rights Reserved

This **LitPlan** for Gary Paulsen's
Hatchet
has been brought to you by Teacher's Pet Publications, Inc.

Copyright Teacher's Pet Publications 1996
11504 Hammock Point
Berlin MD 21811

Only the student materials in this unit plan (such as worksheets,
study questions, and tests) may be reproduced multiple times
for use in the purchaser's classroom.

For any additional copyright questions,
contact Teacher's Pet Publications.

www.tpet.com

TABLE OF CONTENTS - *Hatchet*

Introduction	7
Unit Objectives	10
Unit Outline	11
Reading Assignment Sheet	12
Study Questions	15
Quiz/Study Questions (Multiple Choice)	22
Pre-Reading Vocabulary Worksheets	35
Lesson One (Introductory Lesson)	47
Nonfiction Assignment Sheet	52
Writing Assignment 1	60
Writing Evaluation Form	61
Oral Reading Evaluation Form	63
Writing Assignment 2	67
Writing Assignment 3	69
Extra Writing Assignments/Discussion ?s	71
Vocabulary Review Activities	76
Unit Review Activities	77
Unit Tests	85
Unit Resource Materials	117
Vocabulary Resource Materials	135

A Few Notes About the Author
Gary Paulsen

PAULSEN, Gary 1939- Gary Paulsen was born on May 17, 1939, in Minneapolis, Minnesota. He is a second-generation American. His father's family emigrated to the United States from Denmark, and his mother's family came form Norway and Sweden. Paulsen's father was a career Army officer, and the family moved frequently. He had few friends and did not do well in school. Due to family problems, Paulsen spent much of his growing-up years with his aunts and grandmother. During these years, he was introduced to books by a friendly librarian, and began reading voraciously.

Paulsen attended Bemidjii College from 1957-1958. He paid his tuition by working as a trapper for the state of Minnesota. From 1959-1962 he worked with missiles in the United States Army. Upon his release, he took courses and became a field engineer. He worked as an aerospace field engineer from 1962-1966. During this time he read an article about flight testing and thought getting paid to write about things he liked would be a good way to earn a living.

In order to break into the writing field, Paulsen made up a resume. He was hired as an associate editor by a magazine in Hollywood, California. Although his supervisors realized he had falsified the resume, they were willing to teach him about the writing business and he worked there for one year. He also worked as a film extra and a sculptor.

The Special War was Paulsen's first book. It was based on his interviews with servicemen who had served in the Vietnam War. In the next twelve years he published 40 books, 200 magazine articles, short stories, and two plays. His topics included hunting, trapping, farming, and young adult and adult fiction. Many of the adventures in his books come from his own experiences. Paulsen has sailed alone to Hawaii, lived in the northern wilderness alone with only a bow and arrow, and driven a motorcycle cross country.

After he published *Winterkill* in 1977, he was sued for libel. He won the case after a long battle. By this time he was almost bankrupt and had no desire to write, so he returned to trapping predators for the state of Minnesota. During this time a friend gave him a four dog sled team. He took the dogs on a seven day run. At the end of the run he resigned from his job, determined not to kill any more animals. Next, Paulsen entered the Iditarod, the 1200 mile long dogsled race in Alaska. A publisher gave him the money to enter the race and asked to be the first to see whatever writing Paulsen did after the race.

Paulsen published *Dancing Carl* in 1983. This was originally a narrative ballet for two dancers, and a short version was shown on Minnesota Public Television. He published *Tracker*, the story of a young boy who is hunting alone for the first time after his grandfather's death, in 1984. This was followed by Dogsong in 1985. Paulsen actually wrote Dogsong while training his team for the Iditarod. It is the story of a young Eskimo boy who takes his dog team across Alaska. It was a Newbery Honor Book in 1986. *Hatchet,* the story of a young boy lost in the Canadian wilderness for 54 days with nothing but a hatchet, was named a Newbery Honor book in 1988. Several other books have been chosen as American Library Association

Best Books for Young Adults, Notable Children's books, and National Council of Teachers of English Notable Books in the Language Arts.

One of his current works is *Madonna*, a collection of stories about some of the strong women he has known. Other works include *The Foxman* (1977), *The Spitball Gang* (1980), *The Crossing*, (1987), *The River*, (1991), *The Haymeadow*, (1992), and *Nightjohn,* (1993).

Mr. Paulsen continues to write and lives in Leonard, Minnesota. He also gives public readings and performances near his home.

INTRODUCTION

This unit has been designed to develop students' reading, writing, thinking, listening and speaking skills through exercises and activities related to *Hatchet* by Gary Paulsen. It includes eighteen lessons, supported by extra resource materials.

The **introductory lesson** introduces students to one main theme of the novel, survival in difficult circumstances, through a bulletin board activity. Following the introductory activity, students are given an explanation of how the activity relates to the book they are about to read.

The **reading assignments** are approximately thirty pages each; some are a little shorter while others are a little longer. Students have approximately 15 minutes of pre-reading work to do prior to each reading assignment. This pre-reading work involves reviewing the study questions for the assignment and doing some vocabulary work for four to eight vocabulary words they will encounter in their reading.

The **study guide questions** are fact-based questions; students can find the answers to these questions right in the text. These questions come in two formats: short answer or multiple choice. The best use of these materials is probably to use the short answer version of the questions as study guides for students (since answers will be more complete), and to use the multiple choice version for occasional quizzes. It might be a good idea to make transparencies of your answer keys for the overhead projector.

The **vocabulary work** is intended to enrich students' vocabularies as well as to aid in the students' understanding of the book. Prior to each reading assignment, students will complete a two-part worksheet for approximately four to eight vocabulary words in the upcoming reading assignment. Part I focuses on students' use of general knowledge and contextual clues by giving the sentence in which the word appears in the text. Students are then to write down what they think the words mean based on the words' usage. Part II gives students dictionary definitions of the words and has them match the words to the correct definitions based on the words' contextual usage. Students should then have an understanding of the words when they meet them in the text.

After each reading assignment, students will go back and formulate answers for the study guide questions. Discussion of these questions serves as a **review** of the most important events and ideas presented in the reading assignments.

There are eighteen **Daily Lessons,** which include suggestions for reading the book with the students. There are two minilessons on characterization (Lessons 2 and 9), two on conflict (Lessons 3 and 6), and one on flashback (Lesson 4). These lessons include blackline masters for graphic organizers.

Following the reading of the book, a lesson (Lesson 14) is devoted to the **extra discussion questions/writing assignments**. These questions focus on interpretation, critical analysis and personal response, employing a variety of thinking skills and adding to the students' understanding of the novel. These questions are done as a **group activity**. Using the information they have acquired so far through individual work and class discussions, students get together to further examine the text and to brainstorm ideas relating to the themes of the novel.

The group discussion is followed by a **project** session in which individuals or groups share their ideas about the book with the entire class in the form of art work, dramatizations, writing, and further discussions . Thus, the entire class gets exposed to many different ideas regarding the themes and events of the book.

After students complete extra discussion questions, there is a **vocabulary review** lesson which pulls together all of the separate vocabulary lists for the reading assignments and gives students a review of all of the words they have studied.

There are three **writing assignments** in this unit, each with the purpose of informing, persuading, or having students express personal opinions. The first assignment is to express a personal **opinion**: students will give their views on who should decide where a teenager lives when his/her parents divorce. The second assignment is to **persuade**: students will try to persuade the Canadian government to continue searching for Brian. The third assignment is to **inform**: students will write a newspaper article about finding Brian alive after the plane crash.

In addition, there is a **nonfiction reading assignment**. Students are required to read a piece of nonfiction related in some way to *Hatchet*. After reading their nonfiction pieces, students will fill out a worksheet on which they answer questions regarding facts, interpretation, criticism, and personal opinions. During one class period, students make **oral presentations** about the nonfiction pieces they have read. This not only exposes all students to a wealth of information, it also gives students the opportunity to practice **public speaking**.

The **review lesson** pulls together all of the aspects of the unit. The teacher is given four or five choices of activities or games to use which all serve the same basic function of reviewing all of the information presented in the unit.

The **unit tes**t comes in two formats: all multiple choice-matching-true/false or with a mixture of matching, short answer, and composition. As a convenience, two different tests for each format have been included.

There are additional **support materials** included with this unit. The **resource sections** include suggestions for an in-class library, crossword and word search puzzles related to the novel, and extra vocabulary worksheets. There is a list of **bulletin board ideas** which gives the teacher suggestions for bulletin boards to go along with this unit. In addition, there is a list of **extra class activities** the teacher could choose from to enhance the unit or as a substitution for an exercise the teacher might feel is inappropriate for his/her class. **Answer keys** are located directly after the **reproducible student materials** throughout the unit. The student materials may be reproduced for use in the teacher's classroom without infringement of copyrights. No other portion of this unit may be reproduced without the written consent of Teacher's Pet Publications, Inc.

UNIT OBJECTIVES *Hatchet*

1. Through reading *Hatchet* students will analyze the main character and his situation to better understand the themes of the novel.

2. Students will demonstrate their understanding of the text on four levels: factual, interpretive, critical, and personal.

3. Students will practice reading aloud and silently to improve their skills in each area.

4. Students will enrich their vocabularies and improve their understanding of the novel through the vocabulary lessons prepared for use in conjunction with it.

5. Students will answer questions to demonstrate their knowledge and understanding of the main events and characters in *Hatchet*.

6. Students will practice writing through a variety of writing assignments.

7. The writing assignments in this are geared to several purposes:
    a. To check the students' reading comprehension
    b. To make students think about the ideas presented by the novel
    c. To make students put those ideas into perspective
    d. To encourage critical and logical thinking
    e. To provide the opportunity to practice good grammar and improve students' use of the English language.

8. Students will read aloud, report, and participate in large and small group discussions to improve their public speaking and personal interaction skills.

UNIT OUTLINE *Hatchet*

1	2	3	4	5
Unit Intro Distribute Unit Materials PV 1-3	Minilesson: Characterization R 1-3	Study ?? 1-3 Minilesson: Conflict PVR 4-5	Study ??4-5 Minilesson: Flashback PVR 6-7	Writing Assignment #1
6	7	8	9	10
Study ?? 6-7 Minilesson: Conflict	PVR 8-11 Oral Reading Evaluation Study ??8-11	Quiz 1-11 PVR 12-15	Study ?? 12-15 PVR 16-17 Study ?? 16-17	Writing Conferences Writing Assignment #2
11	12	13	14	15
Minilesson: Characterization PVR 18-Epilogue	Study ?? 18-Epilogue Check Predictions	Writing Assignment #3	Extra Discussion ??	Group Work
16	17	18	19	20
Vocabulary Review	Unit Review	Test	Non-Fiction Assignment Presentations	Movie/ Audio Cassette and Discussion

Key: P = Preview Study Questions   V = Vocabulary Work   R = Read

READING ASSIGNMENT SHEET *Hatchet*

Date to be Assigned	Chapters	Completion Date (Prior to Class on This Date)
	Chapters 1-3	
	Chapters 4-5	
	Chapters 6-7	
	Chapters 8-11	
	Chapters 12-15	
	Chapters 16-17	
	Chapters 18-Epilogue	

STUDY QUESTIONS

SHORT ANSWER STUDY QUESTIONS *Hatchet*

Chapters 1-3

1. Where was Brian going and why?
2. What happened to the pilot?
3. What did Brian do while he was alone in the plane? What happened because of the things he did?
4. What did Brian think his two choices in the plane were? Which did he choose?
5. Describe the plane's landing.

Chapters 4-5

1. What was the part of the Secret that Brian remembered?
2. What was Brian's physical condition?
3. What new disaster happened when the sun came up? What did Brian do about it? Why did it surprise him so much?
4. What things did Brian think about when he woke up from his second sleep?
5. How did thinking about Mr. Perpich help Brian?

Chapters 6-7

1. What did Brain think about that helped him find food and make a shelter?
2. What was Brian's reaction when he saw his reflection in the lake?
3. What did Brian do after his illness from the gut cherries?
4. Describe what Brian did and thought when he saw the bear.

Chapters 8-11

1. What did Brian learn from his encounter with the porcupine?
2. Describe the way Brian made a fire. Tell how he felt about the fire.
3. What new food did Brian find? How did he feel at first about eating it? What did he do with the rest of the food?
4. As he was eating his new food, Brian thought about the searchers. What did he think?
5. What changes did Brian notice in himself?

Chapters 12-15

1. Describe the hunger that Brian felt.
2. Describe the incident with the plane, and how Brian felt after it.
3. On day 47 after the crash, Brian thought about the true and new things, and about tough hope. What were the true and new things? What was tough hope?
4. Describe Brian's encounter with the skunk, and what he learned from it.
5. What was Brian's major breakthrough? How did he do it? Why was it important?
6. How did Brian begin to measure time? Which day was described in Chapter 16?

Short Answer Study Questions *Hatchet*

Chapters 16-17
1. Which animal attacked Brian? What happened to him?
2. What happened as a result of the tornado?
3. Brian was impatient to begin the plane project when he remembered the order in which he had learned to do things. What was the order?
4. What action did Brian take to get to the plane?

Chapters 18-Epilogue
1. How did Brian get into the plane?
2. What happened while Brian was trying to get into the plane? What did he do about it?
3. What happened when Brian saw the pilot?
4. How did finding the rifle change Brian?
5. Describe Brian's rescue.
6. How long was Brian alone on the lake?
7. What were the temporary and permanent changes in Brian?
8. What was life like for Brian and his parents after he was rescued?
9. What did Brian do about the Secret?

ANSWER KEY: SHORT ANSWER STUDY QUESTIONS *Hatchet*

Chapters 1-3

1. Where was Brian going and why?

    He was going from Hampton, New York to Canada to spend the summer with his father. His parents were recently divorced. He lived with his mother for the school year and was going for his first summer visit with his father.

2. What happened to the pilot?

    He had a heart attack while flying the plane. He died.

3. What did Brian do while he was alone in the plane? What happened because of the things he did?

    He tried to fly the plane himself but he didn't understand how to use the instruments. He used the radio to call for help. He made some contact, but then lost it.

4. What did Brian think his two choices in the plane were? Which did he choose?

    He thought his two choices were to wait for the plane to run out of gas or to pull the throttle out and make the plane land. He left the plane running and tried the radio every ten minutes.

5. Describe the plane's landing.

    The engine died suddenly. Brian was able to guide the plane toward a lake. The plane crashed through some trees and landed in a lake. Brian didn't realize that he was screaming as the plane was crashing. Once the plane was in the water, Brian got himself to the surface of the lake and then to the shore, where he passed out.

Chapters 4-5

1. What was the part of the Secret that Brian remembered?

    He saw his mother sitting in a strange car with a man who was not her husband.

2. What was Brian's physical condition?

    He was bruised and had a lot of aches, his forehead was swollen, but he was not severely injured.

3. What new disaster happened when the sun came up? What did Brian do about it? Why did it surprise him so much?

    Brian was attacked by hordes of mosquitoes and small black flies. He sat with his windbreaker pulled up and took it. He almost cried because of the frustration and pain. He was surprised because such hordes of insects were never mentioned in the books he read or in the movies or on the television shows he watched

4. What things did Brian think about when he woke up from his second sleep?
   He realized that he was thirsty, so he went to the lake and took a long drink. He reviewed the plane crash, and thought his parents would be frantic. He thought someone might be looking for him. Then he got hungry. He wondered what they did in the movies when they got hungry.

5. How did thinking about Mr. Perpich help Brian?
   Mr. Perpich had always said to stay positive and on top of things. He told the students they were their own best assets. Brian wondered how to stay positive and think of himself as an asset. This helped Brian get motivated to find food and make a shelter.

Chapters 6-7
1. What did Brain think about that helped him find food and make a shelter?
   He thought about being in the park with his friend, Terry, when they were pretending to be lost in the woods. They had decided a lean-to was the best type of shelter, so Brian decided to make one for himself. Then he remembered a television show about a survival course for air force pilots. One of the women had found a bush with beans on it. He thought there must be berry bushes in the woods.

2. What was Brian's reaction when he saw his reflection in the lake?
   He realized how dirty and ugly he looked, and it frightened him. He cried out of self pity for several minutes.

3. What did Brian do after his illness from the gut cherries?
   He took a small handful of ripe ones and washed them in the lake before he ate them. He realized he should only eat a small amount at a time so that he would not get sick again. Then he separated the remaining cherries into piles of ripe and not ripe ones. After that he went out looking for more food and found some raspberries.

4. Describe what Brian did and thought when he saw the bear.
   At first he didn't do anything but look at the bear. Then, after the bear had gone, he made a sound of fear, and ran in the opposite direction. After he had run about fifty yards he realized the bear was not interested in him, so he went back to the raspberry bushes and continued picking. Later that night he wondered if the bear had been as surprised as he was.

Chapters 8-11
1. What did Brian learn from his encounter with the porcupine?
   He learned the most important rule of survival: feeling sorry for yourself didn't work.

2. Describe the way Brian made a fire. Tell how he felt about the fire.

He realized he could use the hatchet to create a spark. After several unsuccessful tries he got the right combination of materials in his spark nest. He thought about his science class lessons on what made a fire. He realized he had to blow on it to give it oxygen. When he did this he was able to create a fire. He thought of the fire as his friend.

3. What new food did Brian find? How did he feel at first about eating it? What did he do with the rest of the food?
   He discovered a nest of seventeen turtle eggs. At first he found it difficult to eat the egg. After the first one it was easier, and he ate six eggs. They made him realize how hungry he was. He decided to store the rest of the eggs and eat one a day.

4. As he was eating his new food, Brian thought about the searchers. What did he think?
   He realized he had forgotten about them. He also realized that if he forgot about them they might forget about him, and he had to keep hoping he would be rescued.

5. What changes did Brian notice in himself?
   He saw and heard differently. He knew sounds, didn't just hear them. He saw all of the parts of things. His mind and body had connected in a new way.

Chapters 12-15
1. Describe the hunger that Brian felt.
   It was a hunger that made him hunt. He knew it would always be there, even when he had enough food to eat.

2. Describe the incident with the plane, and how Brian felt after it.
   He was busy making a bow when he heard a whining sound. He realized it was the sound of a jet engine. He tried to get a fire going on the top of the bluff, but the plane moved away before he could do it. He felt hopeful while making the fire, but after the plane left, he felt that all hope was gone.

3. On day 47 after the crash, Brian thought about the true and new things, and about tough hope. What were the true and new things? What was tough hope?
   The true and new things were that he was not the same since the plane had passed. The other was that he would not die. He made a new fire and a new bow. He was finally able to catch fish. Tough hope was his hope that he could learn, survive, and take care of himself.

4. Describe Brian's encounter with the skunk, and what he learned from it.
   The skunk was digging up Brian's eggs. Brian threw sand at it and it sprayed Brian, blinding him for two hours. The smell on Brian and in his shelter lasted for over a month. Brian learned to protect his food by placing it out of reach.

5. What was Brian's major breakthrough? How did he do it? Why was it important?
   He made a small pen to hold live fish. It was a major breakthrough because it showed he was planning ahead.

6. How did Brian begin to measure time? Which day was described in Chapter 16?
   He began to use events to measure time and remember events. The day of First Meat was the day he used his bow and spear to kill a foolbird.

Chapters 16-17
1. Which animal attacked Brian? What happened to him?
   A cow moose attacked him and drove him into the lake. When he tried to get out she attacked again. He pretended to be dead until her attention was diverted, then moved slowly on his hands and knees and was able to get back to land. His ribs were badly hurt. After the moose left the area, Brian went back to the lake to get his bow and spear and the dead foolbird.

2. What happened as a result of the tornado?
   The tornado destroyed Brian's shelter and the fire. It scattered his tools. The only thing he had left was the hatchet. The morning after the tornado, Brian saw the tail of the plane sticking out of the water. Later that night he realized that the survival pack was in the plane. He went to sleep thinking about the pack.

3. Brian was impatient to begin the plane project when he remembered the order in which he had learned to do things. What was the order?
   The order was: first food, then thought, then action.

4. What action did Brian take to get to the plane?
   He made a raft of logs and called it Brushpile One.

Chapters 18-Epilogue
1. How did Brian get into the plane?
   He used the hatchet to cut through the aluminum.

2. What happened while Brian was trying to get into the plane? What did he do about it?
   He dropped the hatchet. He dove under the water to get the hatchet back. He was successful on his second attempt.

3. What happened when Brian saw the pilot?
   He saw the pilot's head. All that was left of it was the skull, because the fish had eaten away the rest. He was sick in the water and nearly choked. His legs jerked instinctively and pushed him toward the surface. He was able to settle himself and get on with his work.

4. How did finding the rifle change Brian?
   Before he had the rifle he had to fit in with the woods and animals around him. After he had it, he didn't have to be afraid or understand as much.

5. Describe Brian's rescue.
   One of the items he took from the survival pack was an emergency transmitter. He couldn't figure out how to make it work, so he put it aside while he cooked some of the food in the packs. As he was getting ready to eat he heard and saw a bushplane landing. When the pilot came out of the plane, Brian introduced himself and asked the pilot if he wanted anything to eat.

6. How long was Brian alone on the lake?
   He was there for fifty-four days.

7. What were the temporary and permanent changes in Brian?
   He temporarily lost seventeen percent of his body weight, and later gained back six percent, but he had almost no body fat. He stayed thin for several years. His reactions changed permanently. He was more able to observe situations and react to them. He thought slowly before speaking. He marveled and wondered at food from then on.

8. What was life like for Brian and his parents after he was rescued?
   He was famous for awhile. The Canadian government sent in a recovery team and they gave him copies of the pictures and film they took. He had many dreams about the lake, but they were not disturbing. His parents appeared to be getting back together, but after a week his father went back to the oil fields. His mother still saw the man in the station wagon.

9. What did Brian do about the Secret?
   He kept it a secret, and never told his father about it.

MULTIPLE CHOICE QUESTIONS *Hatchet*

Chapters 1-3

1. Where was Brian going?
    - A. He was going from New York to Canada to spend the summer with his father.
    - B. He was going from California to New York to visit his mother.
    - C. He was going from Canada to Alaska on a camping trip with his father.
    - D. He was going from New York to Hampton, Virginia, to see his grandparents.

2. What happened to the pilot while he was flying the plane?
    - A. He got drunk and passed out.
    - B. He took an overdose of tranquilizers and died.
    - C. He went into a diabetic coma.
    - D. He had a heart attack and died.

3. What did Brian do while he was alone in the plane?
    - A. He passed out from fright.
    - B. He tried to use the radio and broke it in frustration when it didn't work.
    - C. He tried to fly the plane himself and used the radio to call for help.
    - D. He cried and prayed.

4. Which of the following describes what Brian chose to do about the plane?
    - A. He strapped on the parachute and bailed out.
    - B. He waited for the plane to run out of gas.
    - C. He turned off the engine and forced the plane to crash.
    - D. He pulled the throttle out to make the plane land.

5. Which of the following did **not** happen as the plane landed?
    - A. Brian was completely silent as the plane crashed.
    - B. The engine died suddenly.
    - C. The plane crashed through some trees and landed in a lake.
    - D. Brian got himself to the surface of the lake and then to the shore.

Multiple Choice Questions *Hatchet*

<u>Chapters 4-5</u>

1. What was the part of the Secret that Brian remembered?
    A. He found letters his father had written to another woman.
    B. He saw his mother sitting in a strange car with a man who was not her husband.
    C. He heard his father talking on the phone to a woman.
    D. A friend told Brian his mother had been at a movie with a strange man.

2. What was Brian's physical condition?
    A. He had a broken arm and two black eyes.
    B. He had three broken ribs and cuts and bruises on his legs and arms.
    C. He had a concussion and a dislocated shoulder.
    D. He was bruised and had a lot of aches, and his forehead was swollen.

3. What new disaster happened when the sun came up?
    A. Brian was attacked by hordes of mosquitoes and small black flies.
    B. Brian was attacked by a colony of killer ants.
    C. Brian was attacked by a flock of small birds.
    D. Brian went to was in the lake and was attacked by flesh-eating fish.

4. Why did the new disaster surprise him so much?
    A. He was surprised because he thought these things only happened at night.
    B. He was surprised because these things were never mentioned in the books he read or in the movies or on the television shows he watched.
    C. He was surprised because he thought there weren't any of these creatures in the woods.
    D. He was surprised because he thought these creatures were afraid of humans.

5. Which of the following did **not** happen when Brian woke up from his second sleep?
    A. He took a long drink from the lake.
    B. He thought his parents would be frantic.
    C. He tried to make a sling for his arm from a branch and his windbreaker.
    D. He wondered what they did in the movies when they got hungry.

6. Brian remembered something Mr. Perpich had told his class. What was it?
    A. Always think before acting.
    B. Never give in to fear. Act in spite of it.
    C. Visualize where you want to be and do what you have to to get there.
    D. Stay positive and on top of things. The students were their own best assets.

Multiple Choice Questions *Hatchet*

Chapters 6-7

1. What did Brain think about that helped him find food?
    - A. He thought about camping and fishing with his friend, Terry.
    - B. He thought about a book he had read about a man who was stranded on an island and how he found food.
    - C. He thought about a television show about a survival course for air force pilots. One of the women had found a bush with beans on it.
    - D. He thought about his Eagle Scout survival course and finding berries in the woods.

2. What was Brian's reaction when he saw his reflection in the lake?
    - A. He cheered because he was alive.
    - B. He threw a stone to destroy the reflection because he looked so ugly.
    - C. He was excited to see that he was beginning to grow a beard and mustache.
    - D. He cried out of self pity for several minutes.

3. What did Brian do after his illness from the gut cherries?
    - A. He was afraid to eat any more of them so he threw the rest of them out.
    - B. He realized he should only eat a small about at a time so that he would not get sick again.
    - C. He crushed them inside his jacket and drank the juice.
    - D. He ate some grass to help his stomach settle down again.

4. Brian saw a bear close up. Describe what he did after the bear left.
    - A. Brian made a sound of fear, and ran in the opposite direction. Then he realized the bear was not interested in him, so he kept picking raspberries.
    - B. He ran back to his shelter and hid there for two days. He practiced loud yells that he thought would scare the bear.
    - C. He used his hatchet to make a spear to use in case the bear attacked him.
    - D. He lay on the ground and screamed and shook in fear. Then he got up and went to look for berry bushes in another part of the forest.

Multiple Choice Questions *Hatchet*

Chapters 8-11

1. Brian learned the most important rule of survival after the porcupine attacked him. What was it?
    - A. Never to sleep without a weapon in your hand.
    - B. Never throw something in the dark.
    - C. Feeling sorry for yourself didn't work.
    - D. Stay calm no matter what happens.

2. What was the key to making the fire?
    - A. Brian needed a lot of small, dry twigs.
    - B. Brian was trying to make the fire in the shelter, and he should have done it outside.
    - C. Brian realized he could use the hatchet to create a spark.
    - D. Brian remembered he had a lighter in the pocket of his windbreaker.

3. What did he do with the turtle eggs?
    - A. He ate six eggs, then decided to store the rest of the eggs and eat one a day.
    - B. He ate all of them raw.
    - C. He buried them under the coals of the fire and roasted them.
    - D. He left them in the nest because he felt like he was a murderer to take them.

4. What did Brian think about the searchers?
    - A. He thought he should give up because there was no way for them to find him.
    - B. He was sure they would find him, so he didn't think he had to waste time thinking about them. He needed to think about surviving until they found him.
    - C. He thought that if he concentrated hard enough, one of them might feel his thoughts and find him.
    - D. If he forgot about them they might forget about him, and he had to keep hoping he would be rescued.

5. What changes did Brian notice in himself?
    - A. He had grown two inches taller and lost twenty pounds.
    - B. He knew sounds, didn't just hear them. He saw all of the parts of things.
    - C. He was forgetting how to speak because there was no one to talk to.
    - D. He was getting stronger and braver. He felt at home in the forest.

Multiple Choice Questions *Hatchet*

<u>Chapters 12-15</u>

1. Describe the hunger that Brian felt.
    - A. It was a hunger that made him feel sick every time he ate.
    - B. It was a hunger that made him hunt.
    - C. It was a hunger that made him feel thankful for finding even a little bit of food.
    - D. It was a hunger that made him want to eat all of the time.

2. How did Brian feel after he realized the search plane disappeared?
    - A. He felt that all hope was gone.
    - B. He hoped a pilot with sharper eyes would look for him next.
    - C. He was glad, because he was having a good time and didn't want to be rescued.
    - D. He thought the pilot was playing a game with him and would come back soon.

3. Brian thought he could learn, survive, and take care of himself. What did he call this?
    - A. He called it the three laws of living.
    - B. He called it tough hope.
    - C. He called it Brian's assets.
    - D. He called it Mr. Perpich's principles.

4. What did Brian learn from his trouble with the skunk?
    - A. He learned to keep his eyes closed when a skunk was nearby.
    - B. He learned to aim to kill, not to scare.
    - C. He learned to share his food with the animals.
    - D. He learned to protect his food by placing it out of reach.

5. What was Brian's major breakthrough? Why was it important?
    - A. He made a trap to catch foolbirds. He would not have to eat just fish anymore.
    - B. He made a bowl out of clay. Now he would be able to save and store leftovers.
    - C. He made a small pen to hold live fish. It showed he was planning ahead.
    - D. He made a jacket of rabbit skins. He could provide warm clothes for the winter.

6. How did Brian begin to measure time?
    - A. He began to use events to measure time.
    - B. He began to bundle sticks together into groups of seven to show the weeks.
    - C. He used the hatchet to draw a calendar on a piece of bark.
    - D. He named each week after a friend or a relative.

Multiple Choice Questions *Hatchet*

<u>Chapters 16-17</u>

1. What happened to Brian when the moose attacked?
    - A. He killed the moose with his bow and arrow.
    - B. His ribs were badly hurt.
    - C. He was stranded in the middle of the lake overnight.
    - D. The moose bit his leg and it got infected.

2. Which of the following did not happen as a result of the tornado?
    - A. The tornado destroyed Brian's shelter.
    - B. The tornado put out the fire.
    - C. The tornado drove the hatchet deep into a tree trunk.
    - D. The tornado shifted the plane around and it was sticking out of the water.

3. Brian was impatient to begin the plane project when he remembered the order in which he had learned to do things. What was the order?
    - A. The order was: first food, then thought, then action.
    - B. The order was first thought, then food, then action.
    - C. The order was first sleep, then thought, then food.
    - D. The order was first food, then sleep, then thought.

4. How did Brian get to the plane?
    - A. He swam out.
    - B. He built a bridge of logs and walked over it.
    - C. The water was shallow so he walked out to it.
    - D. He made a raft of logs.

Multiple Choice Questions *Hatchet*
<u>Chapters 18-Epilogue</u>

1. How did Brian get into the plane?
    A. He kicked holes in it with his feet.
    B. He went in through the broken windshield.
    C. He used the hatchet to cut through the aluminum.
    D. He threw large stones and made a hole in the side of the plane.

2. What happened while Brian was trying to get into the plane?
    A. He dropped the hatchet into the water.
    B. The plane shifted and he was trapped under a wing.
    C. He cut his arm on a sharp piece of aluminum.
    D. He was attacked by a beaver that thought there was food in the plane.

3. What happened when Brian saw the pilot's head?
    A. He fainted and almost drowned.
    B. He was sick in the water and nearly choked.
    C. He cried and cried.
    D. He realized just how glad he was to be alive.

4. Before he had this item from the plane, Brian had to fit in with the woods and animals around him. After he had it, he didn't have to be afraid or understand as much. What was the item?
    A. It was the lighter.
    B. It was the lamp.
    C. It was the food packs.
    D. It was the rifle.

5. What did Brian do that got him rescued?
    A. He built a large signal fire on top of the bluff.
    B. He made a large SOS from rocks in a clearing.
    C. He accidentally turned on the emergency transmitter from the survival pack.
    D. He shot the rifle and some trappers heard it.

6. How long was Brian alone on the lake?
    A. He was there for thirty-nine days.
    B. He was there for fifty-four days.
    C. He was there for seventy-two days.
    D. He was there for sixty-one days.

Multiple Choice Questions *Hatchet*
Chapter 18-Epilogue

7. Which of these was a temporary change in Brian?
    A. He refused to have his hair cut.
    B. He slept in the back yard for several months.
    C. He lost seventeen percent of his body weight.
    D. He could not stand noises.

8. Which of these was a permanent change in Brian?
    A. He refused to eat packaged foods.
    B. He didn't enjoy talking to people.
    C. He would never fly in a plane again.
    D. He was more able to observe situations and react to them.

9. What happened to Brian's parents after he was rescued?
    A. His parents appeared to be getting back together, but didn't.
    B. They stopped speaking to each other completely.
    C. They agreed to try living together again for six months.
    D. They felt so guilty about Brian's accident that they got back together.

10. What did Brian do about the Secret?
    A. He told his mother and asked for an explanation.
    B. He kept it a secret, and never told his father about it.
    C. The shock of the accident made him forget it completely.
    D. He wrote a letter about it to his father, but never mailed it.

STUDENT ANSWER SHEET-MULTIPLE CHOICE QUIZ/STUDY GUIDE QUESTIONS

Chapters 1-3
1. _____
2. _____
3. _____
4. _____
5. _____

Chapters 4-5
1. _____
2. _____
3. _____
4. _____
5. _____
6. _____

Chapters 6-7
1. _____
2. _____
3. _____
4. _____

Chapters 8-11
1. _____
2. _____
3. _____
4. _____
5. _____

Chapters 12-15
1. _____
2. _____
3. _____
4. _____
5. _____
6. _____

Chapters 16-17
1. _____
2. _____
3. _____
4. _____

Chapter 18-Epilogue
1. _____
2. _____
3. _____
4. _____
5. _____
6. _____
7. _____
8. _____
9. _____

ANSWER KEY-MULTIPLE CHOICE QUIZ/STUDY GUIDE QUESTIONS

Chapters 1-3
1. A
2. D
3. C
4. B
5. A

Chapters 4-5
1. B
2. D
3. A
4. B
5. C
6. D

Chapters 6-7
1. C
2. D
3. B
4. A

Chapters 8-11
1. C
2. C
3. A
4. D
5. B

Chapters 12-15
1. B
2. A
3. B
4. D
5. C
6. A

Chapters 16-17
1. B
2. C
3. A
4. D

Chapter 18-Epilogue
1. C
2. A
3. B
4. D
5. C
6. B
7. C
8. D
9. A
10. B

PREREADING VOCABULARY WORKSHEETS

Prereading Vocabulary Worksheets *Hatchet*

Chapters 1-3

Part I: Using Prior Knowledge and Context Clues

Below are the sentences in which the vocabulary words appear in the text. Read the sentence. Use any clues you can find in the sentence combined with your prior knowledge, and write what you think the underlined words mean on the lines provided.

1. But in five minutes they had leveled off at six thousand feet and headed northwest and from then on the pilot had been silent, staring out the front, and the *drone* of the engine had been all that was left.

    _____

2. Instead his eyes burned and tears came, the *seeping* tears that burned, but he didn't cry.

    _____

3. Brian turned again to glance at the pilot, who had both hands on his stomach and was *grimacing* in pain, reaching for the left shoulder again as Brian watched.

    _____

4. He stopped as a fresh *spasm* of pain hit him.

    _____

5. The pilot did not move except that his head rolled on a neck impossibly loose as the plane hit a small bit of *turbulence*.

    _____

6. This caused the plane to slow dramatically and almost seem to stop and *wallow* in the air.

    _____

7. There was a great *wrenching* as the wings caught the pines at the side of the clearing and broke back, ripping back just outside the main braces.

    _____

Prereading Vocabulary Worksheets *Hatchet*

8. A color came that he had never seen before, a color that exploded in his mind with the pain and he was gone, gone from it all, *spiraling* out into the world, spiraling out into nothing.

_____

Chapters 1-3
Part II: Determining the Meaning   Match the vocabulary words to their dictionary definitions.

_____ 1. drone   A. tearing; slashing
_____ 2. seeping   B. violent, agitated winds
_____ 3. grimacing   C. twisting the face to show pain
_____ 4. spasm   D. roll around
_____ 5. turbulence   E. twisting; winding
_____ 6. wallow   F. a continuous low humming sound
_____ 7. wrenching   G. involuntary muscle contraction
_____ 8. spiraling   H. dripping; trickling

Prereading Vocabulary Worksheets *Hatchet*

Chapters 4-5

Part I: Using Prior Knowledge and Context Clues

Below are the sentences in which the vocabulary words appear in the text. Read the sentence. Use any clues you can find in the sentence combined with your prior knowledge, and write what you think the underlined words mean on the lines provided.

1. When he opened them again it was evening and some of the sharp pain had *abated* -- there were many dull aches -- and the crash came back to him fully.

   _____

2. Worst was a *keening* throb in his head that pulsed with every beat of his heart.

   _____

3. His forehead felt *massively* swollen to the touch, almost like a mound out over his eyes, and it was so tender that when his fingers grazed it he nearly cried.

   _____

4. They would look for him, look for the plane. His father and mother would be *frantic*. They would tear the world apart to find him.

   _____

5. Perpich used to drum that into them -- "You are your most valuable *asset*. Don't forget that. You are the best thing you have."

   _____

Part II: Determining the Meaning Match the vocabulary words to their dictionary definitions.

____	1. abated	A.	intense; piercing
____	2. keening	B.	enormously
____	3. massively	C.	lessened, diminished
____	4. frantic	D.	advantage; resource
____	5. asset	E.	highly excited with emotion or frustration

Prereading Vocabulary Worksheets *Hatchet*

Chapters 6-7

Part I: Using Prior Knowledge and Context Clues

Below are the sentences in which the vocabulary words appear in the text. Read the sentence. Use any clues you can find in the sentence combined with your prior knowledge, and write what you think the underlined words mean on the lines provided.

1. Some of the rock that had been scooped out had also been *pulverized* by the glacial action, turned into sand, and now made a small sand beach that went down to the edge of the water in front and to the right of the overhang.

   _____

2. If only I had matches, he thought, looking *ruefully* at the beach and lakeside.

   _____

3. As soon as the cold water hit his stomach he felt the hunger sharpen, as it had before, and he stood and held his abdomen until the hunger cramps *receded*.

   _____

4. Soon, as before, his stomach was full, but now he had some sense and he did not *gorge* or cram more down.

   _____

Part II: Determining the Meaning   Match the vocabulary words to their dictionary definitions.

_____ 1. pulverized   A. stuff; devour
_____ 2. ruefully   B. ground up; crumbled
_____ 3. receded   C. regretfully
_____ 4. gorge   D. withdrew; went back

Prereading Vocabulary Worksheets *Hatchet*

Chapters 8-11

Part I: Using Prior Knowledge and Context Clues

Below are the sentences in which the vocabulary words appear in the text. Read the sentence. Use any clues you can find in the sentence combined with your prior knowledge, and write what you think the underlined words mean on the lines provided.

1. In the initial *segment* of the dream his father was standing at the side of a living room looking at him and it was clear from his expression that he was trying to tell Brian something.

   _____

2. He settled back on his haunches in *exasperation*, looking at the pitiful clump of grass and twigs.

   _____

3. Where the bark was peeling from the trunks it lifted in tiny *tendrils*, almost fluffs.

   _____

4. He could not leave the fire at first. It was so *precious* to him, so close and sweet a thing, the yellow and red flames brightening the dark interior of the shelter, the happy crackle of the dry wood as it burned, that he could not leave it.

   _____

5. He had decided to always have enough on hand for three days and after spending one night with the fire for a friend he knew what a *staggering* amount of wood it would take.

   _____

Part II: Determining the Meaning Match the vocabulary words to their dictionary definitions.

_____ 1. segment   A. annoyance
_____ 2. exasperation   B. long, slender, curling strands
_____ 3. tendrils   C. overwhelming
_____ 4. precious   D. section; part
_____ 5. staggering   E. of high cost or worth; valuable

Prereading Vocabulary Worksheets *Hatchet*

Chapters 6-7

Part I: Using Prior Knowledge and Context Clues

Below are the sentences in which the vocabulary words appear in the text. Read the sentence. Use any clues you can find in the sentence combined with your prior knowledge, and write what you think the underlined words mean on the lines provided.

1. Some of the rock that had been scooped out had also been *pulverized* by the glacial action, turned into sand, and now made a small sand beach that went down to the edge of the water in front and to the right of the overhang.
   _____

2. If only I had matches, he thought, looking *ruefully* at the beach and lakeside.
   _____

3. As soon as the cold water hit his stomach he felt the hunger sharpen, as it had before, and he stood and held his abdomen until the hunger cramps *receded*.
   _____

4. Soon, as before, his stomach was full, but now he had some sense and he did not *gorge* or cram more down.
   _____

Part II: Determining the Meaning   Match the vocabulary words to their dictionary definitions.

_____ 1. pulverized   A. stuff; devour
_____ 2. ruefully   B. ground up; crumbled
_____ 3. receded   C. regretfully
_____ 4. gorge   D. withdrew; went back

Prereading Vocabulary Worksheets *Hatchet*

7. It was *infuriating*. He would pull the bow back, set the arrow just above the water, and when the fish was no more than an inch away release the arrow. Only to miss.

_____

8. The bow had given him this way and he *exulted* in it, in the bow, in the arrow, in the fish, in the hatchet, in the sky.

_____

Chapters 12-15
Part II: Determining the Meaning Match the vocabulary words to their dictionary definitions.

_____ 1. lunged   A. lifted; heaved
_____ 2. flailing   B. aggravating; maddening
_____ 3. prong   C. enduring; persevering
_____ 4. crude   D. thin, pointed, projecting part
_____ 5. hefted   E. waving or swinging vigorously
_____ 6. persistent   F. rejoiced; delighted
_____ 7. infuriating   G. not carefully or completely made; rough
_____ 8. exulted   H. dashed; charged

Prereading Vocabulary Worksheets *Hatchet*

Chapters 16-17

Part I: Using Prior Knowledge and Context Clues

Below are the sentences in which the vocabulary words appear in the text. Read the sentence. Use any clues you can find in the sentence combined with your prior knowledge, and write what you think the underlined words mean on the lines provided.

1. Not *accurately* -- he never got really good with it -- but fly correctly so that if a rabbit or a foolbird sat in one place long enough, close enough, had he had enough arrows, he could hit it.

   _____

2. He slowed his movements and stood slowly, without stretching *unduly*, and went to the lake for a drink.

   _____

3. He tried wedging them together, crossing them over each other -- nothing seemed to work. And he needed a *stable* platform to get the job done.

   _____

4. And for a moment he was *stymied*. He had no rope, only the bowstring and the other cut shoestring in his tennis shoes -- which were by now looking close to dead, his toes showing at the tops.

   _____

Part II: Determining the Meaning Match the vocabulary words to their dictionary definitions.

_____ 1. accurately   A. excessively
_____ 2. unduly   B. thwarted; stumped
_____ 3. stable   C. correctly
_____ 4. stymied   D. firm, steady

Prereading Vocabulary Worksheets *Hatchet*

Chapter 18-Epilogue

Part I: Using Prior Knowledge and Context Clues

Below are the sentences in which the vocabulary words appear in the text. Read the sentence. Use any clues you can find in the sentence combined with your prior knowledge, and write what you think the underlined words mean on the lines provided.

1. It was *instinctive*, fear more than anything else, fear of what he had seen.

   _____

2. A first aid kit with bandages and tubes of *antiseptic* paste and small scissors.

   _____

3. No speaker, no lights, just a small switch at the top and on the bottom he finally found, in small print: Emergency *Transmitter*.

   _____

4. The pilot who landed so suddenly in the lake was a fur buyer mapping Cree trapping camps for future buying runs -- drawn by Brian when he *unwittingly* turned on the emergency transmitter and left it going.

   _____

5. For a brief time the press made much of Bian and he was interviewed for several networks but the *furor* died within a few months.

   _____

Part II: Determining the Meaning Match the vocabulary words to their dictionary definitions.

____ 1. instinctive   A. natural; intuitive
____ 2. antiseptic   B. not knowing; not intended
____ 3. transmitter   C. an electronic device that sends a signal
____ 4. unwittingly   D. intense excitement
____ 5. furor   E. germ-free; disinfectant

Prereading Vocabulary Worksheets *Hatchet*

ANSWER KEY-PREREADING VOCABULARY WORKSHEETS

Chapters 1-3
1. F
2. H
3. C
4. G
5. B
6. D
7. A
8. E

Chapters 4-5
1. C
2. A
3. B
4. E
5. D

Chapters 6-7
1. B
2. C
3. D
4. A

Chapters 8-11
1. D
2. A
3. B
4. E
5. C

Chapters 12-15
1. H
2. E
3. D
4. G
5. A
6. C
7. B

Chapters 16-17
1. C
2. A
3. C
4. B

Chapter 18-Epilogue
1. A
2. E
3. C
4. B
5. D

DAILY LESSONS

LESSON ONE

Student Objectives
    1. To preview the *Hatchet* Unit
    2. To receive books and other related materials (study guides, reading assignment)
    3. To relate prior knowledge to the new material
    4. To become familiar with the vocabulary for Chapters 1-3
    5. To preview the study questions for Chapters 1-3

Activity #1

    Direct attention to the bulletin board display of wilderness areas. Ask students to describe what they see. Then show pictures of hatchets, or show a toy hatchet. Have students form small groups and brainstorm what they would do if they were alone in the wilderness with only a hatchet. Each group should record their answers on a piece of paper. Invite students to read their ideas aloud. Collect and save the papers until students have finished reading the novel. Tell students that the boy in the story, Brian Robeson, gets stranded in the wilderness with only his hatchet. After they read the novel, they will have the opportunity to compare their answers with what he did to survive.

Activity #2

    Distribute the materials students will use in this unit. Explain in detail how students are to use these materials.

    Study Guides Students should preview the study guide questions before each reading assignment to get a feeling for what events and ideas are important in that section. After reading the section, students will (as a class or individually) answer the questions to review the important events and ideas from that section of the book. Students should keep the study guides as study materials for the unit test.

    Reading Assignment Sheet You need to fill in the reading assignment sheet to let students know when their reading has to be completed. You can either write the assignment sheet on a side blackboard or bulletin board and leave it there for students to see each day, or you can "ditto" copies for each student to have. In either case, you should advise students to become very familiar with the reading assignments so they know what is expected of them.

    Unit Outline You may find it helpful to distribute copies of the Unit Outline to your students so they can keep track of upcoming lessons and assignments. You may also want to post a copy of the Unit Outline on a bulletin board and cross off each lesson as you complete it.

    Extra Activities Center The Unit Resource portion of this unit contains suggestions for a library of related books and articles in your classroom as well as crossword and word search puzzles. Make an extra activities center in your room where you will keep these materials for students to use. Bring the books and articles in from the library and keep several copies of the puzzles on hand. Explain to students that these materials are available for students to use when they finish reading assignments or other class work early.

<u>Books</u> Each school has its own rules and regulations regarding student use of school books. Advise students of the procedures that are normal for your school.

<u>Notebook or Unit Folder</u> You may want the students to keep all of their worksheets, notes, and other papers for the unit together in a binder or notebook. During the first class meeting, tell them how you want them to arrange the folder. Make divider pages for vocabulary worksheets, prereading study guide questions, review activities, notes, and tests. You may want to give a grade for accuracy in keeping the folder.

Activity #3

Do a group KWL Sheet with the students (form included.) Some students will know something about Gary Paulsen or his books and will have information to share. Put this information in the K column (What I Know.) Ask students what they want to find out from reading the book and record this in the W column (What I Want to Find Out.) Keep the sheet and refer back to it after reading the book. Complete the L column (What I Learned) at that time.

Activity #4

Work through the prereading vocabulary worksheet for Chapters 1-3 with the students. Tell them they will have a sheet like this to complete before reading each section of the book.

Activity #5

Show students how to preview the study questions for Chapters 1-3 of *Hatchet*. Encourage students to predict what they think answers might be, to write down their predictions, and to compare these with their answers after reading the chapters.

KWL *Hatchet*

Directions: Before reading, think about what you already know about Gary Paulsen and/or *Hatchet*. Write the information in the K column. Think about what you would like to find out from reading the book. Write your questions in the W column. After you have read the book, use the L column to write the answers to your questions from the W column, and anything else you remember from the book.

K **What I Know**	**W** **What I Want to Find Out**	**L** **What I Learned**

LESSON TWO

Student Objectives
    1. To understand character development by discussing Brian's character
    2. To read Chapters 1-3
    3. To become familiar with the Nonfiction Assignment

Activity #1: Minilesson: Character Development

    Explain that an author creates a character, in this case Brian Robeson, by giving him traits such as physical attributes, thoughts, and feelings. The author develops these traits by telling what the character says, does, and thinks. Writers usually base their characters at least in part on a real person or persons, and then elaborate. (Gary Paulsen actually spent time living in the wilderness alone with only a bow and arrow as survival tools. This experience helped him develop the character of Brian Robeson.) A good writer will make the characters believable for the readers.

    Explain that this is a "coming-of-age" story, or bildungsroman, where the central character becomes more aware of himself because of events that occur. In this novel, the awareness comes because of Brian's experience of survival in the Canadian wilderness.

    Have students look for Brian's character traits as they begin reading. After they have read the first three chapters, help them begin filling in the Character Trait Chart (included.) Tell them they should continue to be aware of Brian's character as they read, and that they will continue the discussion and complete more of the chart during Lesson 8.

Activity #2

    You may want to read Chapter 1 aloud to the students to set the mood for the novel. Invite willing students to read Chapters 2-3 aloud to the rest of the class.

Activity #3

    Distribute copies of the Nonfiction Assignment sheet and go over it in detail with the students. Explain to students that they each are to read at least one nonfiction piece at some time during the unit. This could be a book, a magazine article, or information from an encyclopedia or the Internet. Students will fill out a nonfiction assignment sheet after completing the reading to help you (the teacher) evaluate their reading experiences and to help the students think about and evaluate their own reading experiences. Give them the due date for the assignment (Lesson 12.)

    Encourage students to read about topics that are related to the theme of the novel. Some suggestions are: wilderness survival; physical characteristics of the Canadian wilderness; animals of the Canadian wilderness; tornadoes and their effects; the fur trade in Canada; Cree trapping camps; Native American tribes in Canada; small aircraft; the history of hand tools; survival programs such as Outward Bound; and the effects of divorce on children.

CHARACTER TRAITS CHART *Hatchet*

CHARACTER _____

CHARACTER TRAIT _____ EVENTS THAT SHOW THAT TRAIT:	CHARACTER TRAIT _____ EVENTS THAT SHOW THAT TRAIT:
CHARACTER TRAIT _____ EVENTS THAT SHOW THAT TRAIT:	CHARACTER TRAIT _____ EVENTS THAT SHOW THAT TRAIT:

NONFICTION ASSIGNMENT SHEET *Hatchet*
(To be completed after reading the required nonfiction article)

Name _____ Date _____ Class _____

Title of Nonfiction Read _____

Written By _____ Publication Date _____

I. Factual Summary: Write a short summary of the piece you read.

II. Vocabulary:
    1. Which vocabulary words were difficult?

    2. What did you do to help yourself understand the words?

III. Interpretation: What was the main point the author wanted you to get from reading his/her work?

IV. Criticism:
    1. Which points of the piece did you agree with or find easy to believe? Why?

    2. With which points of the piece did you disagree or find difficult to believe? Why?

V. Personal Response:
    1. What do you think about this piece?

    2. How does this piece help you better understand the novel *Hatchet*?

LESSON THREE

Student Objectives
1. To review the main ideas and themes in Chapters 1-3
2. To identify the types of conflict in the novel
3. To become familiar with the vocabulary for Chapters 4-5
4. To preview the study questions for Chapters 4-5
5. To read Chapters 4-5

Activity #1

Discuss the answers to the Study Guide questions for Chapters 1-3 in detail. Write the answers on the board or overhead projector so students can have the correct answers for study purposes. Encourage students to take notes. If the students own their books, encourage them to use high lighter pens to mark important passages and the answers to the study guide questions.

Note: It is a good practice in public speaking and leadership skills for individuals students to take charge of leading the discussion of the study questions. Perhaps a different student could go to the front of the class and lead the discussion each day that the study questions are discussed during this unit. Of course, the teacher should guide the discussion when appropriate and be sure to fill in any gaps the students leave.

Activity #2 Minilesson: Conflict

Tell students that conflict is one of the most important aspects of a work of fiction. The conflict usually is an obstacle to the main character's goal. It usually brings about some type of change in the main character. The types of conflict that are evident in *Hatchet* are character vs. nature, character vs. character, character vs. himself, and character vs. society.

You may want to use examples from stories the students have previously read, or examples from literature for younger children to illustrate the various types of conflict. Dorothy in *The Wizard of Oz* has a conflict with nature because the tornado takes her away from her home. The conflict between Cinderella and her wicked step-mother is an example of character vs. character. In *The Little Engine That Could*, the little engine is not sure of its ability to take the train over the mountain, illustrating the character vs. himself conflict. The Greek myth of Atalanta illustrates character vs. society or the environment. Atalanta was expected to marry the man her father chose, but she did not wish to do so.

Have students begin filling out the Conflict Chart after they have read Chapters 4-5. Discuss their findings. Encourage them to look for more examples of conflict as they read. Tell them they will discuss conflict again in Lesson Five.

Activity #3

Give students about ten or fifteen minutes to do the prereading vocabulary work and preview the study questions for Chapters 4-5.

Activity #4

Have students begin reading Chapters 4 and 5. Depending on the needs and abilities of your students, either have them read silently or orally.

CONFLICT CHART *Hatchet*

Directions: Use the chart below to record examples of the different types of conflict you read about in *Hatchet*.

CONFLICT	EXAMPLE and PAGES	CHANGE in Brian
CHARACTER VS. NATURE		
CHARACTER VS. SELF		
CHARACTER VS. SOCIETY		
CHARACTER VS. CHARACTER		

LESSON FOUR

Student Objectives
1. To review the main ideas and themes in Chapters 4-5
2. To identify the examples of flashback in the novel
3. To become familiar with the vocabulary for Chapters 6-7
4. To preview the study questions for Chapters 6-7
5. To read Chapters 6-7

Activity #1

Go over the answers to the Study Guide questions for Chapters 4 and 5. Encourage students to skim the chapters to find the correct answers to questions they missed.

Activity #2 Minilesson: Flashback

Flashback is a literary device in which the author inserts a previous event into the current event or scene in the story. It is used to give the reader a better understanding of the character's behavior or motivation in the present. A flashback may take place as a dream or as a memory.
Paulsen uses several instances of flashback throughout the novel to explain the Secret and Brian's upset about his parents' divorce. He also uses flashback to show how Brian used his prior knowledge to think of ways to survive in the wilderness.

You may want to show a visual illustration of how a flashback is used. A clip from a television show or movie that uses a flashback will be effective. You could also draw a picture of Brian in the cockpit of the plane with a thought balloon above his head. The thought balloon contains books with titles such as *How to Fly A Plane, All About Airplanes, Airplane Wings and How They Work.*. Also encourage students to look for clue words such as *thought back to, remembered, reminisced* and *dreamed*.

Have students find the examples of flashback used so far in the novel, and record them on the Flashback Chart. (Chapter 1, Brian receives the hatchet from his mother; Chapter 2, Brain remembers information about planes from books he has read; Chapter 4, the memory of the Secret; Chapter 5, Mr. Perpich.) Encourage them to find and record the examples of flashback in Chapters 6 and 7 after they have read. (Brian and Terry in the park pretending to be lost in the woods; last Thanksgiving; television show about the survival course; his mother and the strange man at Amber Mall.)

Activity #3

Give students about fifteen minutes to preview the study questions for Chapters 6-7 and do the related vocabulary work.

Activity #4

Have students read Chapters 6-7 for the rest of the period.

FLASHBACK CHART *Hatchet*

FLASHBACK (Chapter & Description)	**How it is used in the story**
<u>Chapter 1</u>: Brian is on the plane, thinking about his parent's divorce.	It gives the reader background to understand why Brian is going on his trip. It also introduces one of the conflicts in the story.
<u>Chapter 2</u>	
<u>Chapter 3</u>	
<u>Chapter 4</u>	
<u>Chapter 5</u>	
<u>Chapter 6</u>	
<u>Chapter 7</u>	
<u>Chapter 8</u>	

Chapter 9	
Chapter 10	
Chapter 11	
Chapter 13	
Chapter 14	
Chapter 15	
Chapter 16	

LESSON FIVE

Student Objective
  To write a personal opinion paper

Activity #1
  Write the word *opinion* on the board and ask students what it means. Invite them to give their opinions on topics such as what should be served for lunch in the school cafeteria, if the school should have a dress code, their favorite singer/group. Ask other students to agree or disagree, and state their reasons. Make the point that all people have opinions. A person expressing an opinion should be able to back it up with facts and reasons why he/she has the opinion.

Activity #2
  Distribute copies of Writing Assignment #1. Go over the assignment in detail with the students. Tell them they will have the remainder of the class period to begin working on the assignment. Give the due date for the completed assignment. It should be a few days before the writing conferences, which are scheduled for Lesson 10.

Activity #3
  Distribute copies of the Writing Evaluation Form (included with this Unit Plan.) Explain to students that during Lesson Ten you will be holding individual writing conferences about this writing assignment. Make sure students are familiar with the criteria on the Writing Evaluation Form.

Follow Up: After you have graded the assignments, have a writing conference with each student. This Unit Plan schedules one in Lesson 10. After the writing conference, allow students to revise their papers using your suggestions to complete the revisions. Grade the revisions on an A-C-E scale: A = all revisions well done; C = some revisions made; E = few or no revisions made. This will speed your grading time and still give some credit for the students' efforts.

WRITING ASSIGNMENT #1 *Hatchet*
Writing to Express a Personal Opinion

PROMPT

Brian thinks frequently of his parents' divorce, and the courtroom scene where the judge told him he would live with his mother and visit his father. The reader is not told whether or not Brian was asked to give his opinion on where he should live. You will give your opinion in this paper: Should teenagers be given a choice of where to live if their parents get divorced?

PREWRITING

If your parents are divorced, you will probably already have an opinion on this topic. If they are not divorced, you may want to talk to a friend who lives with one parent and visits the other to find out what the experience is like. You may also want to read about the topic in a magazine, newspaper, or another book. Then form your opinion. Next, brainstorm a list of reasons for your opinion. Decide on the best order for your reasons, and number them on your list.

DRAFTING

Your opening statement should state the topic and give your opinion about it.. Next state your most important reason. Explain your reason with personal experiences or facts about the topic. In the next paragraph, state your next reason and the facts that support it. Write one paragraph for each reason. In your closing paragraph, state your topic and opinion again.

PEER CONFERENCE/REVISING

When you finish the rough draft, ask another student to look at it. You may want to give the student your brainstorm list so he/she can double check for you and see that you have included all of the information. After reading, he or she should tell you what he/she liked best about your opinion paper, which parts were difficult to understand or needed more information, and ways in which your work could be improved. Reread your opinion paper considering your critic's comments and make the corrections you think are necessary.

PROOFREADING/EDITING

Do a final proofreading of your opinion paper, double-checking your grammar, spelling, organization, and the clarity of your ideas.

WRITING EVALUATION FORM *Hatchet*

Name _____ Date _____ Class _____

Writing Assignment # _____

Circle One For Each Item:

Composition	excellent	good	fair	poor
Style	excellent	good	fair	poor
Grammar	excellent	good	fair	poor (errors noted)
Spelling	excellent	good	fair	poor (errors noted)
Punctuation	excellent	good	fair	poor (errors noted)
Legibility	excellent	good	fair	poor (errors noted)

Strengths:

Weaknesses:

Comments/Suggestions:

LESSON SIX

Student Objectives
    1. To review the main ideas and themes in Chapters 6-7
    2. To identify the examples of conflict in the novel
    3. To become familiar with the vocabulary for Chapters 8-11
    4. To preview the study questions for Chapters 8-11

Activity #1

    Have students work with a partner and go over their study guide questions and answers for Chapters 6-7. Then briefly go over the answers with the whole class.

Activity #2 Minilesson: Conflict

    Continue the discussion of conflict in the novel. Have students reread Chapters 4-7 for examples of conflict, and record them on their Conflict Chart. Remind them to do this again after they finish reading Chapters 8-11.

Activity #3

    Use the rest of the period for independent work. Have students do the prereading vocabulary worksheet and study guide questions for Chapters 8-11. If they have time, they can begin reading silently. Tell students their oral reading will be evaluated during the next class period. Suggest they read Chapters 8-11 silently ahead of time, and practice reading some of the paragraphs aloud.

LESSON SEVEN

Student Objectives
    1. To practice correct intonation and expression in oral reading
    2. To read Chapters 8-11 orally for evaluation
    3. To discuss the main ideas and events in Chapters 8-11

Activity #1

    Tell students their oral reading ability will be evaluated. Show them copies of the Oral Reading Evaluation Form and discuss it. Model correct intonation and expression by reading the first few paragraphs of Chapter 8 aloud.

Activity #2

    Call on individual students to read a few paragraphs aloud. Encourage the other students to follow along silently in their books. If you have a student who is unwilling or unable to read in front of the group make arrangements to do his or her evaluation privately at another time.

ORAL READING EVALUATION *Hatchet*

Name_____ Class_____ Date_____--

SKILL	EXCELLENT	GOOD	AVERAGE	FAIR	POOR
Fluency	5	4	3	2	1
Clarity	5	4	3	2	1
Audibility	5	4	3	2	1
Pronunciation	5	4	3	2	1
_____	5	4	3	2	1
_____	5	4	3	2	1

Total _____ Grade _____

Comments:

LESSON EIGHT

Student Objectives
    1. To take a quiz on Chapters 1-11
    2. To become familiar with the vocabulary for Chapters 12-15
    4. To preview the study questions for Chapters 12-15
    5. To read Chapters 12-15

Activity #1

    Quiz--distribute quizzes (multiple choice study questions for Chapters 1-11) and give students about fifteen minutes to complete them. Collect the papers for scoring and recording the grades.

Activity #2

    Give students about fifteen minutes to do the prereading vocabulary worksheet and study guide questions for Chapters 12-15. You may want to let them work with a partner or in small groups for this activity.

Activity #3

    Remind students to think about the conflicts and character development as they are reading. Have students read the chapters aloud or silently, depending on their needs and abilities. You may want to let the quicker students read ahead silently while you conduct an oral reading of the story with the students who need more guidance.

LESSON NINE

Student Objectives
1. To review the main ideas and themes in Chapters 12-15
2. To become familiar with the vocabulary for Chapters 16-17
3. To read Chapters 16-17
4. To review the main ideas and events in Chapters 16-17

Activity # 1

Give each student four 1"x2" strips of colored paper or index cards--one blue, one yellow, one green, one pink. Have them put a large letter A on the blue paper, B on the yellow, C on the green, and D on the pink. Distribute copies of the Multiple Choice/Quiz questions for Chapters 12-15. Ask students to read the first question and hold up the colored paper for the correct answer. Then have them mark the correct answer on their worksheets.

Activity #2

Give students ten or fifteen minutes to do the prereading vocabulary worksheet for Chapters 16-17.

Activity #3

Put the prereading questions for Chapters 16-17 on the board or on an overhead transparency. Ask students to choose one question they would like to answer after reading. Group the students according to their choices. Have each group prepare the answer to their question after they have read the text. They may give the answer by reading the information from the text, summarizing it, or dramatizing the event.

Activity #4

Use the rest of the class time for reading the chapters and discussing the answers to the study guide questions.

LESSON TEN

Student Objectives
    1. To write a persuasive essay
    2. To participate in a writing conference with the teacher
    3. To revise Writing Assignment #1 based on the teacher's suggestions

Activity #1

    Distribute copies of Writing Assignment #2. Discuss it in detail and make sure the students understand what to do. Allow the rest of the class period for students to work on the assignment.

    You may want to let students work with a partner or a small group for this assignment. If so, make sure they understand that they will all receive the same grade.

Activity #3

    Choose a quiet corner of the room and hold the individual writing conferences.

LESSON ELEVEN

Student Objectives
    1. To identify the examples of characterization in the novel
    2. To become familiar with the vocabulary for Chapter 18-Epilogue
    3. To preview the study questions for Chapter 18-Epilogue
    4. To read Chapter 18-Epilogue

Activity #1 Minilesson: Characterization

    Ask students to tell you everything they remember about characterization from the previous lessons. Record their answers on the board. Then ask them to think about the ways Brian has changed since the beginning of the novel. Have them support their answers with examples from the novel. Let them work individually or in small groups to add to the Character Trait Chart. Tell students to look for further evidence of changes in Brian in the last two chapters.

Activity #2

    Give students a few minutes to complete the prereading vocabulary worksheet.

Activity #3

    Have students predict the answers to the study guide questions before they read. When they are finished, have them compare their answers with the events in the book.

Activity #4

    Let students begin reading the chapters in the time remaining. Remind them that the reading must be completed before the next class meeting.

WRITING ASSIGNMENT #2 *Hatchet*
Writing to Persuade

PROMPT

The Canadian government stopped looking for Brian and the plane two months before he was found. You think they should have kept searching. You have organized a group of Brian's friends and relatives who feel as you do. They have asked you to present their request for an extended search to the government. You are now preparing that request, and will present it at the next government meeting.

PREWRITING

Make a list of the reasons you and your group want the search to continue. Think of statements to support each of your reasons, and list them under each reason. Then number the reasons in order from most to least important.

DRAFTING

Make an introductory statement in which you describe Brian, the reason he was flying to Canada, and your knowledge of what happened. Then briefly outline what has been done so far to find him. Next, state your request.

Use one paragraph for each of your reasons. Use the supporting statements for each reason.

Summarize your request and respectfully ask for a reply from the government by a certain date, possibly a week after the meeting.

PEER CONFERENCING/REVISING

When you finish the rough draft, ask another student to look at it. You may want to give the student your checklist so he/she can double check for you and see that you have included all of the information. After reading, he or she should tell you what he/she liked best about your persuasive speech, which parts were difficult to understand or needed more information, and ways in which your work could be improved. Reread your persuasive speech considering your critic's comments and make the corrections you think are necessary.

PROOFREADING/EDITING

Do a final proofreading of your persuasive speech, double-checking your grammar, spelling, organization, and the clarity of your ideas.

LESSON TWELVE

Student Objectives
    1. To review the main ideas and events in Chapter 18-Epilogue
    2. To compare predictions made at the beginning of the novel with actual events
    3. To complete all previous assignments

Activity #1
    Invite students to give the answers for the study guide questions. Discuss the accuracy of their earlier predictions.

Activity #2
    On the board, list the ideas for survival that the students thought of at the beginning of the unit. Circle any that Brian actually used. Then write the rest of Brian's survival techniques next to the ones already on the board.

Activity #3
    Use the rest of the class period to have students go through their notes and worksheets and check to see that all work has been completed.

Activity #4
    If students have completed all assignments and there is extra class time, choose one of the Unit Review activities in Lesson 17 and do it now.

LESSON THIRTEEN

Student Objective
    To write a news article based on the novel.

Activity #1
    Show students several newspaper articles about accidents or people who have been missing and then found. Review the basic parts of a news article.

Activity #2
    Distribute copies of Writing Assignment #3. Discuss it in detail. Allow students to use the rest of the class period to work on the writing assignment. Give them a due date for the final draft.

Publishing Suggestions
    1. Use a computer publishing program and publish final drafts in the form of a class newspaper.
    2. Have students use poster board or 11"x17' paper to create a news article. They could include a picture to go along with the article. Display the completed projects on a bulletin board.

WRITING ASSIGNMENT #3 *Hatchet*
Writing to Inform

PROMPT

After Brian was rescued, the press was very interested in him. You are a new, young newspaper reporter. You have convinced your boss to let you show what you can do by interviewing Brian and writing an article for the newspaper. She agrees, and you get your big chance.

PREWRITING

A news article must answer six basic questions: **Who** is the story about?; **What** happened?; **When** did it happen?; **Where** did it happen?; **Why** did it happen?; **How** did it happen? Before you interview Brian, make a list of the questions you want to ask him. Then reread the novel to find the answers to your questions. Once you have answered the 5W and H questions, decide on their order of importance for your article. Number them on your list. Make a list of these questions on a sheet of paper.

DRAFTING

Write a rough draft of your news article. Check your list to make sure you have included all of the information. Make sure you put the most important information from your list first in the story. Then create the headline. The headline tells the main idea of the story. It usually includes who is in the story and what happened. A headline does not have to be a complete sentence, but it should have a powerful verb. Read some headlines in your local newspaper to get the idea before you write yours. Next, put your byline and dateline on the news article. The byline is the name of the writer. It goes under the headline, on the right side of the page. The dateline is the date and place where the story took place. It goes on the first line of the story, before the story begins.

PROMPT

When you finish the rough draft, ask another student to look at it. You may want to give the student your notes so he/she can double check for you and see that you have included all of the information. After reading, he or she should tell you what he/she liked best about your news article, which parts were difficult to understand or needed more information, and ways in which your work could be improved. Reread your news article considering your critic's comments and make the corrections you think are necessary.

LESSON FOURTEEN

<u>Student Objective</u>

    To discuss *Hatchet* at the interpretive and critical levels

<u>Activity #1</u>

    Choose the questions from the Extra Writing Assignments/Discussion Questions which seem most appropriate for your students. A class discussion of these questions is most effective if students have been given the opportunity to formulate answers to the questions prior to the discussion. To this end, you may either have all the students formulate answers to all the questions, divide the class into groups and assign one or more questions to each group, or you could assign one question to each student in your class. The option you choose will make a difference in the amount of class time needed for this activity.

<u>Activity #2</u>

    After students have had ample time to formulate answers to the questions, begin your class discussion of the questions and the ideas presented by the questions. Be sure students take notes during the discussion so they have information to study for the unit test.

EXTRA WRITING ASSIGNMENT/DISCUSSION QUESTIONS *Hatchet*

<u>Interpretation</u>

1. From what point of view is the story written? How does this affect our understanding of the story?

2. What are the main conflicts in the story? Are they resolved? If so, how? If not, why not?

3. What is the setting? How important is the setting to the story? Why?

4. Write a character sketch of Brian Robeson.

5. Why was the Secret so disturbing to Brian?

6. Why did Brian's mother give him the hatchet?

7. Everything in Brian rebelled against stopping the engine and letting the plane fall. Why do you think this was so?

8. Why was Brian so excited about his First Meat?

9. After the tornado had moved off, Brian thought about it hitting the moose. What does this thought show about Brian?

10. Is there a significance to the color amber in the Amber Mall? If so, what is it?

11. Which seemed harder for Brian to deal with, the battle between his parents or his battle for survival?

12. Why do you think Brian reacted the way he did when he was rescued?

13. What was the greatest danger that Brian faced? Why do you think so?

14. Why/how did having the rifle change Brian?

Extra Discussion Questions *Hatchet*

<u>Critical</u>
15. Is the story believable? Why or why not?

16. How did Brian change over the course of the novel? Were these changes for the better?

17. Was the character of Brian believable?

18. Paulsen often used vivid language to describe a scene or event. Give an example of his use of vivid language that you found most effective. Tell why it was effective.

19. What was the overall mood of the story? Give examples to support your answer.

20. Identify a few of the examples of personification and discuss their contribution to the novel.

21. Discuss the role of the hatchet.

22. What is the role/importance of the Secret?

<u>Personal Response</u>
23. Did you enjoy reading *Hatchet*? Why or why not?

24. Is *Hatchet* a good title for the book? Why or why not? If not, what title would you suggest?

25. What do you think Brian will do next?

26. If you were Brian, what would you do about the Secret?

27. If you were Brian's friend or counselor, what would you tell him to do about the Secret?

28. Will you read more of Gary Paulsen's books? Why or why not?

29. Before you read the story, did you think it would be possible to survive in the wilderness alone? What do you think after reading the story?

30. Did Brian's experiences change the way you look at yourself? How?

31. Have you read any other stories similar to *Hatchet*? If so, tell about them.

QUOTATIONS *Hatchet*
Discuss the significance of the following quotations.

1. Divorce. It was an ugly word, he thought. A tearing ugly word that meant fights and yelling, lawyers. . . and the breaking and shattering of all solid things. His home, his life--all the solid things. Divorce. A breaking word, an ugly breaking word.

2. "It's not as complicated as it looks. Good plane like this almost flies itself."

3. "Aches and pains--must be getting old."

4. "Just like a scout. My little scout."

5. He was stopped. Inside he was stopped. He could not think past what he saw, what he felt. All was stopped. The very core of him, the very center of Brian Robeson was stopped and stricken with a white-flash of horror, a terror so intense that his breathing, his thinking, and nearly his heart had stopped.

6. "I am in a plane with a pilot who is--who has had a heart attack or something. He is -- he can't fly. And I don't know how to fly. Help me. Help. . . "

7. Going to die, gonna die, gonna die -- his whole brain screamed it in the sudden silence.

8. I'm alive. It could have been different. There could have been death. I could have been done.

9. He frowned. No, wait -- if he was going to play the game, might as well play it right. Perpich would tell him to quit messing around. Get motivated. Look at *all* of it, Robeson.

10. Simple. Keep it simple. I am Brian Robeson. I have been in a plane crash. I am going to find some food. I am going to find berries.

11. So fast, he thought. So fast things change. When he'd gone to sleep he had satisfaction and in just a moment it was all different.

12. I can't take it this way, alone with no fire and in the dark, and next time it might be something worse, maybe a bear, and it wouldn't be just quills in the leg, it would be worse. I can't do this, he thought, again and again. I can't.

13. "Hello, fire."

14. He had forgotten to think about them and that wasn't good. He had to keep thinking of them because if he forgot them and did not think of them they might forget about him. And he had to keep hoping.

15. Maybe it was always that way, discoveries happened because they needed to happen.

16. Look back and see the smoke now and turn, please turn.

17. He had done food.

18. "Fresh fish," he had yelled. "I have fresh fish for sale."

19. Looking wrong, he thought. I am looking wrong.

20. Patience, he thought. So much of this was patience -- waiting and thinking and doing things right. So much of all this, so much of all living was patience and thinking.

21. But there is a difference no, he thought -- there really is a difference. I might be hit but I'm not done. When the light comes I'll start to rebuild. I still have the hatchet and that's all I had in the first place.

22. He did not know if he would ever get out of this, could not see how it might be, but if he did somehow get home and go back to living the way he had lived would it be just the opposite? Would he be sitting watching television and suddenly think about the sunset up in back of the ridge and wonder how the color looked in the lake?

23. He had done it. That's all he could think now. He had done it.

24. "My name is Brian Robeson. . . Would your like something to eat?"

LESSON FIFTEEN

Student Objectives
    1. To extend the story by means of a project
    2. To work cooperatively in a group

Activity #1

    Allow students to choose one of the following projects. Give them the class period to complete it. If students need more time, you can assign the project as homework or add another day onto the unit plan.

PROJECT IDEAS

1. Draw a book jacket that summarizes the story.

2. Write a critique of the book.

3. Make a timeline showing the important events from the story.

4. Make a diorama showing one of the scenes from the book.

5. Make clay models of the animals in the book.

6. Make puppets and write a puppet show to illustrate one scene from the story.

7. Write a radio or television commercial to advertise the book.

8. Design a poster to advertise the book.

9. Write a different ending to the story.

10. Make a comic book version of the story to share with younger readers.

11. Make a mobile showing the main character, secondary characters and setting.

13. Create a "Missing Person" poster describing Brian.

14. Create a poster showing wilderness survival techniques.

15. Make a collage based on scenes from the book.

LESSON SIXTEEN

Student Objective
    To review all of the vocabulary work done in this unit

VOCABULARY REVIEW ACTIVITIES

1. Divide your class into two teams and have an old-fashioned spelling or definition bee.

2. Give individuals or groups of students a *Hatchet* Vocabulary Word Search Puzzle. The person (group) to find all of the vocabulary words in the puzzle first wins.

3. Give students a *Hatchet* Vocabulary Word Search Puzzle without the word list. The person or group to find the most vocabulary words in the puzzle wins.

4. Put a *Hatchet* Vocabulary Crossword Puzzle onto a transparency on the overhead projector and do the puzzle together as a class.

5. Give students a *Hatchet* Vocabulary Matching Worksheet to do.

6. Use words from the word jumble page and have students spell them correctly.

7. Have students write a story in which they correctly use as many vocabulary words as possible. Have students read their compositions orally. Post the most original compositions on your bulletin board.

8. Have students work in teams and play charades with the vocabulary words.

9. Select a word of the day and encourage students to use it correctly in their writing and speaking vocabulary.

10. Have a contest to see which students can find the most vocabulary words used in other sources. You may want to have a bulletin board available so the students can write down their word, the sentence it was used in, and the source.

11. Assign a word to each student, or let them choose a word. Have them look up the origin of the word, the part of speech, definition, a synonym, and an antonym. Then have them write a sentence using the word. Have students present their information orally to the class, or have them design a word map on paper and display the papers.

LESSON SEVENTEEN

Objective
  To review the main ideas presented in *Hatchet*

Activity #1
  Choose one of the review games/activities included in the packet and spend your class period as outlined there.

Activity #2
  Remind students of the date for the Unit Test. Stress the review of the Study Guides and their class notes as a last minute, brush-up review for homework.

REVIEW GAMES / ACTIVITIES

1. Ask the class to make up a unit test for *Hatchet*. The test should have 4 sections: multiple choice, true/false, short answer and essay. Students may use 1/2 period to make the test, including a separate answer sheet, and then swap papers and use the other 1/2 class period to take a test a classmate has devised. (open book)

2. Take 1/2 period for students to make up true and false questions (including the answers). Collect the papers and divide the class into two teams. Draw a big tic-tac-toe board on the chalk board. Make one team X and one team O. Ask questions to each side, giving each student one turn. If the question is answered correctly, that student's team's letter (X or O) is placed in the box. If the answer is incorrect, no mark is placed in the box. The object is to get three marks in a row like tic-tac-toe. You may want to keep track of the number of games won for each team.

3. Take 1/2 period for students to make up questions (true/false and short answer). Collect the questions. Divide the class into two teams. You'll alternate asking questions to individual members of teams A & B (like in a spelling bee). The question keeps going from A to B until it is correctly answered, then a new question is asked. A correct answer does not allow the team to get another question. Correct answers are +2 points; incorrect answers are -1 point.

4. Allow students time to quiz each other (in pairs) from their study guides and class notes.

5. Give students a *Hatchet* crossword puzzle to complete.

REVIEW GAMES / ACTIVITIES

6. Divide your class into two teams. Use the *Hatchet* crossword words with their letters jumbled as a word list. Student 1 from Team A faces off against Student 1 from Team B. You write the first jumbled word on the board. The first student (1A or 1B) to unscramble the word wins the chance for his/her team to score points. If 1A wins the jumble, go to student 2A and give him/her a clue. He/she must give you the correct word which matches that clue. If he/she does, Team A scores a point, and you give student 3A a clue for which you expect another correct response. Continue giving Team A clues until some team member makes an incorrect response. An incorrect response sends the game back to the jumbled-word face off, this time with students 2A and 2B. Instead of repeating giving clues to the first few students of each team, continue with the student after the one who gave the last incorrect response on the team.

7. Take on the persona of "The Answer Person." Allow students to ask any question about the book. Answer the questions, or tell students where to look in the book to find the answer.

8. Students may enjoy playing charades with events from the story. Select a student to start. Give him/her a card with a scene or event from the story. Allow the players to use their books to find the scene being described. The first person to guess each charade performs the next one.

9. Play a categories-type quiz game. (A master is included in this Unit Plan). Make an overhead transparency of the categories form. Divide the class into teams of three or four players each. Have each team Choose a recorder and a banker. Choose a team to go first. That team will choose a category and point amount. Ask the question to the entire class.(Use the Study Guide Quiz and Vocabulary questions.) Give the teams one minute to discuss the answer and write it down. Walk around the room and check the answers. Each team that answers correctly receives the points. (Incorrect answers are not penalized; they just don't receive any points). Cross out that square on the playing board. Play continues until all squares have been used. The winning team is the one with the most points. You can assign bonus points to any square or squares you choose.

10. Have individual students draw scenes from the book. Display the scenes and have the rest of the class look in their books to find the chapter or section that is being depicted. The first student to find the correct scene then displays his or her picture. When the game is over, collect the pictures and put them in a binder for students to look at during their free time.

NOTE: If students do not need the extra review, omit this lesson and go on to the test.

QUIZ GAME *Hatchet*

Chapters 1-3	Chapters 4-7	Chapters 8-11	Chapters 12-15	Chapters 16-Epilogue
100	100	100	100	100
200	200	200	200	200
300	300	300	300	300
400	400	400	400	400
500	500	500	500	500

LESSON EIGHTEEN

Objective
To test the students' understanding of the main ideas and themes in *Hatchet*

Activity #1
Distribute the *Hatchet* Unit Tests. Go over the instructions in detail and allow the students the entire class period to complete the exam.

Activity #2
Collect all test papers and assigned books prior to the end of the class period.

NOTES ABOUT THE UNIT TESTS IN THIS UNIT:

There are 5 different unit tests which follow.

There are two short answer tests which are based primarily on facts from the novel. The answer key for short answer unit test 1 follows the student test. The answer key for short answer test 2 follows the student short answer unit test 2.

There is one advanced short answer unit test. It is based on the extra discussion questions. Use the matching key for short answer unit test 2 to check the matching section of the advanced short answer unit test. There is no key for the short answer questions. The answers will be based on the discussions you have had during class.

There are two multiple choice unit tests. Following the two unit tests, you will find an answer sheet on which students should mark their answers. The same answer sheet should be used for both tests; however, students' answers will be different for each test. Following the students' answer sheet for the multiple choice tests you will find your answer keys.

The short answer tests have a vocabulary section. You should choose 10 of the vocabulary words from this unit, read them orally and have the students write them down. Then, either have students write a definition or use the words in sentences. The second part of the vocabulary test is matching.

LESSON NINETEEN

Objectives
1. To widen the breadth of students' knowledge about the topics discussed or touched upon in *Hatchet*
2. To check students' non-fiction assignments.

Activity
Ask each student to give a brief oral report about the nonfiction work he/she read for the nonfiction assignment. Your criteria for evaluating this report will vary depending on the level of your students. You may wish for students to give a complete report without using notes of any kind, or you may want students to read directly from a written report, or you may want to do something in between these two extremes. Just make students aware of your criteria in ample time for them to prepare their reports.

Start with one student's report, After that, ask if anyone else in the class has read on a topic related to the first student's report. If no one has, choose another student at random. After each report, be sure to ask if anyone has a report related to the one just completed. That will help keep a continuity during the discussion of the reports.

LESSON TWENTY

Objectives
1. To watch a movie version of the novel *Hatchet*
2. To compare and contrast the movie with the novel

Activity #1
The movie version of *Hatchet* is called *A Cry in the Wild.* It is available in many video stores, and through educational film distributors. Show the movie in class. Note: Since the movie version differs somewhat from the book, it is recommended to show it after giving the test.

Activity #2
Discuss the ways in which the movie and the novel were similar and different. Discuss the reasons for the differences. You may want the students to write a short comparison/contrast paper after this discussion, or record their observations on a Venn Diagram chart.

Note: If your students enjoyed reading *Hatchet,* you may want to have them read *The River*, which is the sequel to *Hatchet*. In *The River*, Brian returns to the wilderness with a government psychologist who wants to study Brian's survival methods. When the man is struck by lightning, and lapses into a coma, Brian must find a way to transport him a hundred miles down the river to a trading post.

UNIT TESTS

SHORT ANSWER UNIT TEST 1 *Hatchet*

I. Matching/ Identify

____ 1. fur buyer
____ 2. Mrs. Robeson
____ 3. Mr. Robeson
____ 4. Mr. Perpich
____ 5. Canada
____ 6. New York
____ 7. porcupine
____ 8. moose
____ 9. skunk
____ 10. foolbird

A. gave the hatchet to Brian
B. blinded Brian for two hours
C. where plane started out
D. drove Brian into the water
E. First Meat
F. where plane went down
G. told students to value themselves
H. attack helped Brian learn to create fire
I. worked in the oil fields
J. rescued Brian

II. Short Answer

1. Describe the way Brian made a fire. Tell how he felt about the fire.

2. What happened as a result of the tornado?

Hatchet Short Answer Unit Test 1

3. What was the Secret? What did Brian decide to do about it?

4. Discuss the importance of the following quotation: "He was stopped. Inside he was stopped. He could not think past what he saw, what he felt. All was stopped. The very core of him, the very center of Brian Robeson, was stopped and stricken white a white-flash of horror, a terror so intense that his breathing, his thinking, and nearly his heart had stopped."

5. Discuss the importance of the following quotation: "My name is Brian Robeson. Would you like something to eat?"

Hatchet Short Answer Unit Test 1

III. Fill-In-the -Blank
1. Brian Robeson was on a plane trip to stay with his father when the pilot _____ and the plane crashed.

2. Brian survived, but lived alone in the wilderness for _____ days.

3. He made a _____ to protect himself.

4. The first food Brain found was _____. He ate too much and got sick.

5. Brian realized he could use his _____ to make a spark, and he created a fire.

6. He always felt a _____ that made him hunt.

7. After the skunk took his turtle eggs, Brain learned to _____ his food.

8. A _____ destroyed Brian's shelter and the fire.

9. Brian was able to get the _____ _____ from the plane.

10. He accidentally turned on the _____ _____ and was rescued.

Hatchet Short Answer Unit Test 1

IV. Essay
What are the main conflicts in the story? Are they resolved? If so, how? If not, why not?

Hatchet Short Answer Unit Test 1

V. Vocabulary Part 1

Listen to the vocabulary words and spell them. After you have spelled all the words, go back and write down the definitions.

WORD **DEFINITION**

1. _____ _____
2. _____ _____
3. _____ _____
4. _____ _____
5. _____ _____
6. _____ _____
7. _____ _____
8. _____ _____
9. _____ _____
10. _____ _____

Vocabulary Part 2   Directions: Place the letter of the matching definition on the blank line.

_____ 1. grimacing   A. overwhelming
_____ 2. frantic   B. aggravating; maddening
_____ 3. pulverized   C. highly excited with emotion or frustration
_____ 4. staggering   D. natural; intuitive
_____ 5. crude   E. enduring; persevering
_____ 6. infuriating   F. intense excitement
_____ 7. persistent   G. ground up; crumbled
_____ 8. stymied   H. twisting the face to show pain
_____ 9. instinctive   I. thwarted; stumped
_____ 10. furor   J. not carefully made; rough

ANSWER KEY SHORT ANSWER UNIT TEST 1 *Hatchet*

I. Matching/ Identify

J	1.	fur buyer	A.	gave the hatchet to Brian
A	2.	Mrs. Robeson	B.	blinded Brian for two hours
I	3.	Mr. Robeson	C.	where plane started out
G	4.	Mr. Perpich	D.	drove Brian into the water
F	5.	Canada	E.	First Meat
C	6.	New York	F.	where plane went down
H	7.	porcupine	G.	told students to value themselves
D	8.	moose	H.	attack helped Brian learn to create fire
B	9.	skunk	I.	worked in the oil fields
E	10.	foolbird	J.	rescued Brian

II. Short Answer

1. Describe the way Brian made a fire. Tell how he felt about the fire.

    He realized he could use the hatchet to create a spark. After several unsuccessful tries he got the right combination of materials in his spark nest. He thought about his science class lessons on what made a fire. He realized he had to blow on it to give it oxygen. When he did this he was able to create a fire. He thought of the fire as his friend.

2. What happened as a result of the tornado?

    The tornado destroyed Brian's shelter and the fire. It scattered his tools. The only thing he had left was the hatchet. The morning after the tornado, Brian saw the tail of the plane sticking out of the water. Later that night he realized that the survival pack was in the plane. He went to sleep thinking about the pack.

3. What was the Secret? What did Brian decide to do about it?

    Brian had seen his mother kissing a strange man in a car near the Amber Mall. He was sure this was the reason his mother wanted the divorce, but his father did not know about it. Brian decided to keep his knowledge to himself.

4. Discuss the importance of the following quotation: "He was stopped. Inside he was stopped. He could not think past what he saw, what he felt. All was stopped. The very core of him, the very center of Brian Robeson, was stopped and stricken with a while-flash of horror, a terror so intense that his breathing, his thinking, and nearly his heart had stopped."

    Brian was in the plane and had just realized that the pilot was dead. He began to understand that he was alone.

5. Discuss the importance of the following quotation: "My name is Brian Robeson. Would you like something to eat?"

   Brian had retrieved the survival pack from the downed plane. He had unwittingly turned on the Emergency Transmitter. He was cooking a huge feast from the food supplies in the survival pack when a fur trapper in a bushplane with floats landed. The trapper recognized Brian as the lost boy from the plane crash. Brian stood looking at the trapper with is tongue stuck to the roof of his mouth. Then he spoke to the pilot.

III. Fill-In-the -Blank
1. Brian Robeson was on a plane trip to stay with his father when the pilot **died of a heart attack** and the plane crashed.
2. Brian survived, but lived alone in the wilderness for **54** days.
3. He made a **shelter of branches** to protect himself.
4. The first food Brain found was **gut-cherries**. He ate too much and got sick.
5. Brian realized he could use his **hatchet** to make a spark, and he created a fire.
6. He always felt a **hunger** that made him hunt.
7. After the skunk took his turtle eggs, Brain learned to **protect** his food.
8. A **tornado** destroyed Brian's shelter and the fire.
9. Brian was able to get the **survival pack** from the plane.
10. He accidentally turned on the **emergency transmitter** and was rescued.

V. Vocabulary Part 1 Choose words from the vocabulary list to read orally for this section.

Vocabulary Part 2

H	1.	grimacing	A.	overwhelming
C	2.	frantic	B.	aggravating; maddening
G	3.	pulverized	C.	highly excited with emotion or frustration
A	4.	staggering	D.	natural; intuitive
J	5.	crude	E.	enduring; persevering
B	6.	infuriating	F.	intense excitement
E	7.	persistent	G.	ground up; crumbled
I	8.	stymied	H.	twisting the face to show pain
D	9.	instinctive	I.	thwarted; stumped
F	10.	furor	J.	not carefully made; rough

SHORT ANSWER UNIT TEST 2 *Hatchet*

I. Matching/Identify

____ 1.	Canada	A.	where plane started out
____ 2.	Mr. Robeson	B.	told students to value themselves
____ 3.	moose	C.	where plane went down
____ 4.	foolbird	D.	blinded Brian for two hours
____ 5.	Mr. Perpich	E.	First Meat
____ 6.	fur buyer	F.	rescued Brian
____ 7.	porcupine	G.	drove Brian into the water
____ 8.	skunk	H.	gave the hatchet to Brian
____ 9.	New York	I.	attack helped Brian learn to create fire
____ 10.	Mrs. Robeson	J.	worked in the oil fields

II. Short Answer

1. Describe the events that happened in the plane. Include what happened to the pilot and what Brian did.

2. On day 47 after the crash, Brian thought about the true and new things, and about tough hope. What were the true and new things. What was tough hope?

Short Answer Unit Test 2 *Hatchet*

3. Describe what Brian did to get into the plane.

4. Discuss the significance of the following quotation: "Hello, fire."

5. Describe the significance of the following quotation: "Fresh fish, I have fresh fish for sale."

Short Answer Unit Test 2 *Hatchet*

III. Fill-In-the-Blank

1. Brian Robeson was on a plane trip to stay with his _____ when the pilot had a heart attack and the plane crashed.

2. He survived, but lived alone in the _____ for 54 days.

3. Brian's first two thoughts were to get _____ and _____.

4. He figured out what to do by thinking about the things he and his friend _____ used to do and by remembering something he saw on television.

5. Brian realized he could use his _____ to make a spark, and he created a fire.

6. Even when he had food, Brian always felt a hunger that made him _____.

7. After the skunk took his turtle eggs, Brain put his food _____.

8. After the tornado hit, Brian knew he would _____.

9. Brian found the survival pack in the _____.

10. He accidentally turned on the emergency transmitter and was rescued by a _____.

IV. Essay

How did Brian change over the course of the novel?

Short Answer Unit Test 2 *Hatchet*

V. Vocabulary Part 1

Listen to the vocabulary words and spell them. After you have spelled all the words, go back and write down the definitions.

WORD	DEFINITION
1. _____	_____
2. _____	_____
3. _____	_____
4. _____	_____
5. _____	_____
6. _____	_____
7. _____	_____
8. _____	_____
9. _____	_____
10. _____	_____

Vocabulary Part 2   Directions: Place the letter of the matching definition on the blank line.

_____ 1. unwittingly   A. dashed; charged
_____ 2. accurately   B. not knowing; not intended
_____ 3. unduly   C. intense; piercing
_____ 4. flailing   D. excessively
_____ 5. lunged   E. with regret
_____ 6. exasperation   F. waving or swinging vigorously
_____ 7. precious   G. stuff; devour
_____ 8. ruefully   H. annoyance
_____ 9. gorge   I. correctly
_____ 10. keening   J. of high cost or worth; valuable

ANSWER KEY SHORT ANSWER UNIT TEST 2 *Hatchet*

I. Matching/Identify

C	1.	Canada	A.	where plane started out
J	2.	Mr. Robeson	B.	told students to value themselves
G	3.	moose	C.	where plane went down
E	4.	foolbird	D.	blinded Brian for two hours
B	5.	Mr. Perpich	E.	First Meat
F	6.	fur buyer	F.	rescued Brian
I	7.	porcupine	G.	drove Brian into the water
D	8.	skunk	H.	gave the hatchet to Brian
A	9.	New York	I.	attack helped Brian learn to create fire
H	10.	Mrs. Robeson	J.	worked in the oil fields

II. Short Answer

1. Describe the events that happened in the plane. Include what happened to the pilot and what Brian did.

    The pilot had a heart attack while flying the plane. He died. Brian tried to fly the plane himself but he didn't understand how to use the instruments. He used the radio to call for help. He made some contact, but then lost it. Brian thought his two choices were to wait for the plane to run out of gas or to pull the throttle out and make the plane land. He left the plane running and tried the radio every ten minutes. The engine died suddenly. Brian was able to guide the plane toward a lake. The plane crashed through some trees and landed in a lake. Brian didn't realize that he was screaming as the plane was crashing. Once the plane was in the water, Brian got himself to the surface of the lake and then to the shore, where he passed out.

2. On day 47 after the crash, Brian thought about the true and new things, and about tough hope. What were the true and new things? What was tough hope?

    The true and new things were that he was not the same since the plane had passed. The other was that he would not die. He made a new fire and a new bow. He was finally able to catch fish. Tough hope was his hope that he could learn, survive, and take care of himself.

3. Describe what Brian did to get into the plane.

    He made a raft of logs and called it Brushpile One. He pushed the raft out to the plane. He used the hatchet to cut through the aluminum skin of the plane, and was able to get inside.

4. Discuss the significance of the following quotation: "Hello, fire."
   When the porcupine attacked Brian, he threw his hatchet at it. The hatchet missed the porcupine, but made sparks against the rock. He had a dream in which his father was trying to tell him something, and then Terry was lighting a charcoal fire in a barbecue pit. When he woke up, he went outside to stretch with the hatchet in his hand. The sun light hit the hatchet and Brian realized he could use it to start a fire. After several attempts he was successful. Then he said, "Hello, fire."

5. Describe the significance of the following quotation: "Fresh fish, I have fresh fish for sale."
   Brian had made a holding pen for live fish, using piles of stone and a willow mesh for the gate. This was a major breakthrough because he was starting to think ahead.

III. Fill-In-the-Blank
1. Brian Robeson was on a plane trip to stay with his **father** when the pilot had a heart attack and the plane crashed.
2. He survived, but lived alone in the Canadian **wilderness** for 54 days.
3. Brian's first two thoughts were to get **food** and **shelter**.
4. He figured out what to do by thinking about the things he and his friend **Terry** used to do and by remembering something he saw on television.
5. Brian realized he could use his **hatchet** to make a spark, and he created a fire.
6. Even when he had food, Brian always felt a hunger that made him **hunt.**
7. After the skunk took his turtle eggs, Brain put his food **on a high ledge**.
8. After the tornado hit, Brian knew he would **rebuild**.
9. Brian found the survival pack **in the plane**.
10. He accidentally turned on the emergency transmitter and was rescued by a **fur trapper**.

V. Vocabulary Part 1 Choose words from the vocabulary list to read orally for this section.

Vocabulary Part 2

B	1.	unwittingly	A.	dashed; charged
I	2.	accurately	B.	not knowing; not intended
D	3.	unduly	C.	intense; piercing
F	4.	flailing	D.	excessively
A	5.	lunged	E.	with regret
H	6.	exasperation	F.	waving or swinging vigorously
J	7.	precious	G.	stuff; devour
E	8.	ruefully	H.	annoyance
G	9.	gorge	I.	correctly
C	10.	keening	J.	of high cost or worth; valuable

ADVANCED SHORT ANSWER UNIT TEST *Hatchet*

I. Matching/Identify

_____ 1. Canada   A. where plane started out
_____ 2. Mr. Robeson   B. told students to value themselves
_____ 3. moose   C. where plane went down
_____ 4. foolbird   D. blinded Brian for two hours
_____ 5. Mr. Perpich   E. First Meat
_____ 6. fur buyer   F. rescued Brian
_____ 7. porcupine   G. drove Brian into the water
_____ 8. skunk   H. gave the hatchet to Brian
_____ 9. New York   I. attack helped Brian learn to create fire
_____ 10. Mrs. Robeson   J. worked in the oil fields

II. Short Answer

1. What are the main conflicts in the story, and how are they resolved?

2. How did Brian change over the course of the novel?

Advanced Short Answer Unit Test *Hatchet*

3. What was The Secret, and why was it so disturbing to Brian?

4. Is the story believable? Why or why not?

5. Identify a few examples of personification in the novel and discuss their contribution to it.

Advanced Short Answer Unit Test *Hatchet*

III. Quotations   Discuss the significance of the following quotations.

1. "Just like a scout. My little scout.

2. "I am in a plane with a pilot who is - who has had a heart attack or something. He is -- he can't fly. And I don't know how to fly. Help me. Help me."

3. He had forgotten to think about them and that wasn't good. He had to keep thinking of them because if he forgot them and did not think of them they might forget about him. And he had to keep hoping.

4. Look back and see the smoke now and turn, please turn.

5. He had done it. That's all he could think now. He had done it.

Advanced Short Answer Unit Test *Hatchet*

IV. Vocabulary

Listen to the words and write them down. After you have written down all of the words, write a paragraph in which you use all of the words. The paragraph must in some way relate to *Hatchet*.

1. _____
2. _____
3. _____
4. _____
5. _____
6. _____
7. _____
8. _____
9. _____
10. _____

MULTIPLE CHOICE UNIT TEST 1 *Hatchet*

I. Matching/ Identify

____	1.	fur buyer	A.	gave the hatchet to Brian
____	2.	Mrs. Robeson	B.	blinded Brian for two hours
____	3.	Mr. Robeson	C.	where plane started out
____	4.	Mr. Perpich	D.	drove Brian into the water
____	5.	Canada	E.	First Meat
____	6.	New York	F.	where plane went down
____	7.	porcupine	G.	told students to value themselves
____	8.	moose	H.	its attack helped Brian create fire
____	9.	skunk	I.	worked in the oil fields
____	10.	foolbird	J.	rescued Brian

II. Multiple Choice

1. What happened to the pilot while he was flying the plane?
    - A. He got drunk and passed out.
    - B. He took an overdose of tranquilizers and died.
    - C. He went into a diabetic coma.
    - D. He had a heart attack and died.

2. Which of the following did **not** happen as the plane landed?
    - A. Brian was completely silent as the plane crashed.
    - B. The engine died suddenly.
    - C. The plane crashed through some trees and landed in a lake.
    - D. Brian got himself to the surface of the lake and then to the shore.

3. Why did the new disaster with the mosquitoes surprise Brian so much?
    - A. He was surprised because he thought these things only happened at night.
    - B. He was surprised because these things were never mentioned in the books he read or in the movies or on the television shows he watched.
    - C. He was surprised because he thought there weren't any of these creatures in the woods.
    - D. He was surprised because he thought these creatures were afraid of humans.

Multiple Choice Unit Test 1 *Hatchet*

4. What did Brain think about that helped him find food?
    A. He thought about camping and fishing with his friend, Terry.
    B. He thought about a book he had read about a man who was stranded on an island and how he found food.
    C. He thought about a television show about a survival course for air force pilots. One of the women had found a bush with beans on it.
    D. He thought about his Eagle Scout survival course and finding berries in the woods.

5. Brian saw a bear close up. Describe what he did after the bear left.
    A. Brian made a sound of fear, and ran in the opposite direction. Then he realized the bear was not interested in him, so he kept picking raspberries.
    B. He ran back to his shelter and hid there for two days. He practiced loud yells that he thought would scare the bear.
    C. He used his hatchet to make a spear to use in case the bear attacked him.
    D. He lay on the ground and screamed and shook in fear. Then he got up and went to look for berry bushes in another part of the forest.

6. What was the key to making the fire?
    A. Brian needed a lot of small, dry twigs.
    B. Brian was trying to make the fire in the shelter, and he should have done it outside.
    C. Brian realized he could use the hatchet to create a spark.
    D. Brian remembered he had a lighter in the pocket of his windbreaker.

7. What changes did Brian notice in himself?
    A. He had grown two inches taller and lost twenty pounds.
    B. He knew sounds, didn't just hear them. He saw all of the parts of things.
    C. He was forgetting how to speak because there was no one to talk to.
    D. He was getting stronger and braver. He felt at home in the forest.

8. Brian thought he could learn, survive, and take care of himself. What did he call this?
    A. He called it the three laws of living.
    B. He called it tough hope.
    C. He called it Brian's assets.
    D. He called it Mr. Perpich's principles.

Multiple Choice Unit Test 1 *Hatchet*

9. What was Brian's major breakthrough? Why was it important?
    A. He made a trap to catch foolbirds. He would not have to eat just fish anymore.
    B. He made a bowl out of clay. Now he would be able to save and store leftovers.
    C. He made a small pen to hold live fish. It showed he was planning ahead.
    D. He made a jacket of rabbit skins. He could provide warm clothes for the winter.

10. What did Brian do that resulted in his rescue?
    A. He built a large signal fire on top of the bluff.
    B. He made a large SOS from rocks in a clearing.
    C. He accidentally turned on the emergency transmitter from the survival pack.
    D. He shot the rifle and some trappers heard it.

III. Quotations Directions: Match the quotation and with its missing word or phrase.

_____ 1.	It was an ugly word, he thought.	A.	fire
_____ 2.	"See how it looks on your belt. Just like a _____."	B.	patience
_____ 3.	There could have been death. I could have been ___.	C.	hatchet
_____ 4.	Perpich would tell him to _____.	D.	done
_____ 5.	"Hello, ____."	E.	divorce
_____ 6.	_____ happened because they needed to happen.	F.	quit messing around
_____ 7.	So much of this was _____.	G.	not done
_____ 8.	I might be hit but I'm ___.	H.	something to eat
_____ 9.	I still have the ___ at that's all I had in the first place.	I.	scout
_____ 10.	"My name is Brian Robeson. Would you like ___?"	J.	discoveries

Multiple Choice Unit Test 1 *Hatchet*

IV. Vocabulary Part 1   Directions: Place the letter of the matching definition on the blank line.

____	1. grimacing	A.	overwhelming
____	2. frantic	B.	aggravating; maddening
____	3. pulverized	C.	highly excited with emotion or frustration
____	4. staggering	D.	natural; intuitive
____	5. crude	E.	enduring; persevering
____	6. infuriating	F.	intense excitement
____	7. persistent	G.	ground up; crumbled
____	8. stymied	H.	twisting the face to show pain
____	9. instinctive	I.	thwarted; stumped
____	10. furor	J.	not carefully made; rough

Vocabulary Part 2   Directions: Circle the letter next to the word that matches the definition.

1. **germ-free; disinfectant**
    a. pulverized
    b. crude
    c. antiseptic
    d. instinctive

2. **annoyance**
    a. spasm
    b. exasperation
    c. segment
    d. prong

3. **involuntary muscle contraction**
    a. wrenching
    b. spasm
    c. tendrils
    d. flailing

4. **section; part**
    a. asset
    b. crude
    c. segment
    d. stable

5. **thin, pointed, projecting part**
    a. prong
    b. stable
    c. antiseptic
    d. drone

6. **violent, agitated winds**
    a. wallow
    b. tendrils
    c. gorge
    d. turbulence

7. **with regret**
    a. exulted
    b. ruefully
    c. crude
    d. unwittingly

8. **dripping; trickling**
    a. pulverized
    b. seeping
    c. infuriating
    d. persistent

9. **excessively**
    a. unduly
    b. massively
    c. accurately
    d. precious

10. **electronic signal sender**
    a. furor
    b. transmitter
    c. asset
    d. tendrils

MULTIPLE CHOICE UNIT TEST 2 *Hatchet*

I. Matching/Identify

___ 1. Canada
___ 2. Mr. Robeson
___ 3. moose
___ 4. foolbird
___ 5. Mr. Perpich
___ 6. fur buyer
___ 7. porcupine
___ 8. skunk
___ 9. New York
___ 10. Mrs. Robeson

A. where plane started out
B. told students to value themselves
C. where plane went down
D. blinded Brian for two hours
E. First Meat
F. rescued Brian
G. drove Brian into the water
H. gave the hatchet to Brian
I. its attack helped Brian create fire
J. worked in the oil fields

II. Multiple Choice

1. What did Brian do while he was alone in the plane?
    A. He passed out from fright.
    B. He looked in the pilot's gear for a guidebook telling how to fly the plane.
    C. He tried to fly the plane himself and used the radio to call for help.
    D. He cried and prayed.

2. Which of the following describes what Brian chose to do about the plane?
    A. He strapped on the parachute and bailed out.
    B. He waited for the plane to run out of gas.
    C. He turned off the engine and forced the plane to crash.
    D. He pulled the throttle out to make the plane land.

3. What was Brian's physical condition?
    A. He had a broken arm and two black eyes.
    B. He had three broken ribs and cuts and bruises on his legs and arms.
    C. He had a concussion and a dislocated shoulder.
    D. He was bruised and had a lot of aches, and his forehead was swollen.

4. Which of the following did **not** happen when Brian woke up from his second sleep?
    A. He took a long drink from the lake.
    B. He thought his parents would be frantic.
    C. He tried to make a sling for his arm from a branch and his windbreaker.
    D. He wondered what they did in the movies when they got hungry.

Multiple Choice Unit Test 2 *Hatchet*

5. What was Brian's reaction when he saw his reflection in the lake?
    A. He cheered because he was alive.
    B. He threw a stone to destroy the reflection because he looked so ugly.
    C. He was excited to see that he was beginning to grow a beard and mustache.
    D. He cried out of self pity for several minutes.

6. Brian learned the most important rule of survival after the porcupine attacked him. What was it?
    A. Never to sleep without a weapon in your hand.
    B. Never throw something in the dark.
    C. Feeling sorry for yourself didn't work.
    D. Stay calm no matter what happens.

7. What was the key to making the fire?
    A. Brian needed a lot of small, dry twigs.
    B. Brian was trying to make the fire in the shelter, and he should have done it outside.
    C. Brian realized he could use the hatchet to create a spark.
    D. Brian remembered he had a lighter in the pocket of his windbreaker.

8. Describe the hunger that Brian felt.
    A. It was a hunger that made him feel sick every time he ate.
    B. It was a hunger that made him hunt.
    C. It was a hunger that made him feel thankful for finding even a little bit of food.
    D. It was a hunger that made him want to eat all of the time.

9. Brian was impatient to begin the plane project when he remembered the order in which he had learned to do things. What was the order?
    A. The order was: first food, then thought, then action.
    B. The order was first thought, then food, then action.
    C. The order was first sleep, then thought, then food.
    D. The order was first food, then sleep, then thought.

10. What did Brian do about the Secret?
    A. He told his mother and asked for an explanation.
    B. He kept it a secret, and never told his father about it.
    C. The shock of the accident made him forget it completely.
    D. He wrote a letter about it to his father, but never mailed it.

Multiple Choice Unit Test 2 *Hatchet*

III. Quotations   Directions: Match the quotation and with its missing word or phrase.

_____ 1. The core of him was stopped and stricken with ___.   A. a white flash of horror
_____ 2. Get _____. Look at all of it, Robeson.   B. food
_____ 3. And he had to keep ____.   C. patience
_____ 4. _____ happened because they needed to happen.   D. motivated
_____ 5. He had done _____.   E. fish
_____ 6. "Fresh ___. I have fresh _____ for sale."   F. something to eat
_____ 7. Looking _____, he thought. I am looking ____.   G. discoveries
_____ 8. So much of all living was _____ and thinking.   H. rebuild
_____ 9. When the light comes I'll start to _____.   I. hoping
_____ 10. "My name is Brian Robeson. Would you like ___?"   J. wrong

IV. Vocabulary Part 1   Directions: Place the letter of the matching definition on the blank line.

_____ 1. unwittingly   A. dashed; charged
_____ 2. accurately   B. not knowing; not intended
_____ 3. abated   C. intense; piercing
_____ 4. flailing   D. lessened; diminished
_____ 5. lunged   E. withdrew; went back
_____ 6. wallow   F. waving or swinging vigorously
_____ 7. precious   G. stuff; devour
_____ 8. receded   H. roll around
_____ 9. gorge   I. correctly
_____ 10. keening   J. of high cost or worth; valuable

Multiple Choice Unit Test 2 *Hatchet*

<u>Vocabulary Part 2</u> Directions: Circle the letter next to the word that matches the definition.

1. **a continuous low humming sound**
    a. wallow
    b. keening
    c. drone
    d. segment

2. **twisting; winding**
    a. grimacing
    b. spiraling
    c. stymied
    d. infuriating

3. **enduring; persevering**
    a. exulted
    b. persistent
    c. antiseptic
    d. unduly

4. **lifted; heaved**
    a. stymied
    b. abated
    c. exulted
    d. hefted

5. **overwhelming**
    a. seeping
    b. grimacing
    c. staggering
    d. instinctive

6. **tearing; slashing**
    a. wrenching
    b. seeping
    c. staggering
    d. infuriating

7. **enormously**
    a. massively
    b. antiseptic
    c. frantic
    d. ruefully

8. **advantage; resource**
    a. instinctive
    b. transmitter
    c. stable
    d. asset

9. **long, slender, curing strands**
    a. prong
    b. spasm
    c. tendrils
    d. segments

10. **rejoiced; delighted**
    a. exulted
    b. persistent
    c. asset
    d. crude

ANSWER SHEET   Multiple Choice Unit Tests *Hatchet*

I. Matching	III. Quotations	IV. Vocabulary
1. _____	1. _____	1. _____
2. _____	2. _____	2. _____
3. _____	3. _____	3. _____
4. _____	4. _____	4. _____
5. _____	5. _____	5. _____
6. _____	6. _____	6. _____
7. _____	7. _____	7. _____
8. _____	8. _____	8. _____
9. _____	9. _____	9. _____
10. _____	10. _____	10. _____

II. Multiple Choice

1. (A) (B) (C) (D)
2. (A) (B) (C) (D)
3. (A) (B) (C) (D)
4. (A) (B) (C) (D)
5. (A) (B) (C) (D)
6. (A) (B) (C) (D)
7. (A) (B) (C) (D)
8. (A) (B) (C) (D)
9. (A) (B) (C) (D)
10. (A) (B) (C) (D)

Part 2

1. _____
2. _____
3. _____
4. _____
5. _____
6. _____
7. _____
8. _____
9. _____
10. _____

ANSWER SHEET KEY   Multiple Choice Unit Test 1 *Hatchet*

I. Matching	III. Quotations	IV. Vocabulary
1. J	1. E	1. H
2. A	2. I	2. C
3. I	3. D	3. G
4. G	4. F	4. A
5. F	5. A	5. J
6. C	6. J	6. B
7. H	7. B	7. E
8. D	8. G	8. I
9. B	9. C	9. D
10. E	10. H	10. F

Part 2
1. C
2. B
3. B
4. C
5. A
6. D
7. B
8. B
9. A
10. B

II. Multiple Choice
1. (A) (B) (C) ( )
2. ( ) (B) (C) (D)
3. (A) ( ) (C) (D)
4. (A) (B) ( ) (D)
5. ( ) (B) (C) (D)
6. (A) (B) ( ) (D)
7. (A) ( ) (C) (D)
8. (A) ( ) (C) (D)
9. (A) (B) ( ) (D)
10. (A) (B) ( ) (D)

ANSWER SHEET KEY Multiple Choice Unit Test 2 *Hatchet*

I. Matching	III. Quotations	IV. Vocabulary
1. C	1. A	1. B
2. J	2. D	2. I
3. G	3. I	3. D
4. E	4. G	4. F
5. B	5. B	5. A
6. F	6. E	6. H
7. I	7. J	7. J
8. D	8. C	8. E
9. A	9. H	9. G
10. H	10. F	10. C

Part 2
1. C
2. B
3. B
4. D
5. C
6. A
7. A
8. D
9. C
10. A

II. Multiple Choice
1. (A) (B) ( ) (D)
2. (A) ( ) (C) (D)
3. (A) (B) (C) ( )
4. (A) (B) ( ) (D)
5. (A) (B) (C) ( )
6. (A) (B) ( ) (D)
7. (A) (B) ( ) (D)
8. (A) ( ) (C) (D)
9. ( ) (B) (C) (D)
10. (A) ( ) (C) (D)

UNIT RESOURCES

BULLETIN BOARD IDEAS *Hatchet*

1. Save one corner of the board for the best of students' *Hatchet* writing assignments. You may want to use background maps of New York and Canada to represent the setting of the novel.

2. Take one of the word search puzzles from the extra activities packet and with a marker copy it over in a large size on the bulletin board. Write the clue words to find to one side. Invite students prior to and after class to find the words and circle them on the bulletin board.

3. Have students find or draw pictures that they think resemble the people and scenery in the book.

4. Invite students to help make an interactive bulletin board quiz. Give each student a half-sheet of paper (about 4"x5') folded in half so that it can open. On the outside flap, have each student write a description of one of the characters in the text. On the inside, they will write the name of the character. You can staple or tack these papers to the bulletin board so that the students can read the descriptions and lift the flaps to find the answers.

5. Collect and display pictures of the Canadian wilderness.

6. Display articles about people who have survived alone in wilderness areas.

7. Display pictures and descriptions of small airplanes and hand tools.

8. Display articles about Gary Paulsen.

9. Have students design postcards depicting the settings of the book.

10. Display a large map of New York state through Canada and have students mark the route that Brian's plane may have taken.

EXTRA ACTIVITIES *Hatchet*

One of the difficulties in teaching a novel is that all students don't read at the same speed. One student who likes to read may take the book home and finish it in a day or two. Sometimes a few students finish the in-class assignments early. The problem, then, is finding suitable extra activities for students.

One thing that helps is to keep a little library in the classroom. For this unit on *Hatchet* you might check out from the school or public library other books by Gary Paulsen. There are also many other survival and coming-of-age novels that students would enjoy reading. Magazines such as *Boy's Life* and *National Geographic World* contain articles about wilderness areas and young adults who do interesting things. Several journals have critiques of Paulsen's works. Some of the students may enjoy reading these and responding either in writing or in discussion groups.

Your students who have reading difficulties, or speak English as a second language may benefit from listening to all or part of the book on tape. *Hatchet* is available commercially, or you may want to have an adult or a student who reads well tape record the book for you.

Other things you may keep on hand are word search puzzles. Several puzzles relating directly to *Hatchet* are included in the unit. Feel free to duplicate them.

Some students may like to draw. You might devise a contest or allow some extra-credit grade for students who draw characters or scenes from *Hatchet*. Note, too, that if the students do not want to keep their drawings you may pick up some extra bulletin board materials this way. If you have a contest and you supply the prize. You could, possibly, make the drawing itself a non-refundable entry fee.

Have maps, a globe, and travel brochures on hand for easy reference. Travel agencies and automobile clubs are good sources for these materials.

The pages which follow contain games, puzzles, and worksheets. The keys, when appropriate, immediately follow the puzzle or worksheet. There are two main groups of activities: one group for for the unit; that is, generally relating to the *Hatchet* text, and another group of activities realated strictly to the *Hatchet* vocabulary.

Directions for the games, puzzles, and worksheets are self-explanatory. The object here is to provide you with extra materials you may use in any way you choose.

MORE ACTIVITIES *Hatchet*

1. Pick one of the incidents for students to dramatize. Encourage students to write dialog for the characters. (Perhaps you could assign various stories to different groups of students so more than one story could be acted and more students could participate.)

2. Have students design a bulletin board (ready to be put up; not just sketched) for *Hatchet*

3. Invite a Scout troop leader or an older Scout to talk to the class about wilderness survival.

4. If you live near a military base, you may be able to have someone from the base come and talk about their survival training.

5. Ask someone from the Red Cross or the local paramedics to talk to the class about survival techniques.

6. Help students design and produce a talk show. Choose one of the story incidents as the topic. The host will interview the various characters. (Students should make up the questions they want the host to ask the characters.)

7. Have students work in pairs to create an interview with one of the characters. One student should be the interviewer and the other should be the interviewee. Students can work together to compose questions for the interviewer to ask. Each pair of students could present their interview to the class.

8. Invite students who have read other books by Gary Paulsen to present booktalks to the class.

9. Invite students who have read a biography of Gary Paulsen to tell the class about his life.

10. Use some of the related topics (noted earlier for an in-class library) as topics for research, reports, or written papers, or as topics for guest speakers.

11. Invite a story teller to tell one or more stories related to *Hatchet* to the class.

12. Invite someone who has lived in one of the areas mentioned in the book to speak to the class.

13. Have students hold small group discussions related to topics in the book. Assign a recorder and a speaker for each group. Have the speaker from each group make a report to the class.

14. Have students work in small groups to write a sequel telling what happened to Brian after he returned from his ordeal.

15. Have students write a survival plan of their own. This could be based on any natural or man-made disaster.

UNIT WORD SEARCH *Hatchet*

All the words in this list are associated with *Hatchet* with emphasis on the characters and events being studied in the unit. The words are placed backwards, forward, diagonally, up and down. The clues below the word search will help identify the words.

```
D P P C E T N G H F E K B W I C Y F A S K W W A M J C Z H K
X R D Y U O K Q G M C J F W E Y B D T F B N C R L L F V R C
L J P V S L H I L L E Y G X X R A S D V C P H Q D C A J R A
L M O T X I A P H K J H G T D N C R I Z U X V G O X M E H P
S K K X J P N W G B P D M A A O B U T V I P X Z D I Y P E L
K J K B J N R Y J H S U O C G H Q U R P H L E W D W J A M A
U L X P L X W B K K X N E W Y O R K L G D F O U S C G W W V
P U R E Y U B R U F E J L A R T H X W G M R W I A O K P V I
K J L K X H B A K J G U L A L E Q L Z H Q U S V R R Z L S V
A C Q S J W I F K D E G E E A T T T T T F H M U U C N J E R
C Z P I E O I S U L G B V R E A F T G S S B O T E Z W O X U
D T A J E C M M M V E S T O Y J E H G A S F L O T Y U N R S
I J I M L A R O V N V A I Y O H R Q G E I J V R M G D K G L
D E X U E Z O E K Y T H O U C G J E W N Q Q W N L Q L B H C
G N F R Y S A M T T D J Y T T R K F U A I V S A F A D C D X
R X D N E G R U A F X Z A A B M D Q U D C S M D J M E X C M
S F M C N J D C N X P H K C I P M N E X G B S O O Y Z X O C
E N D T M J K Q S X J P R H U Y D N O P X M V F N L I Y X B
D X B F E P O H H G U O T F B Z J Z F N M F Z A T T R Z G B
```

BEAR	FUR BUYER	SURVIVAL PACK
CANADA	HATCHET	SECRET
NEW YORK	HEART ATTACK	TORNADO
DREAMS	PILOT	MOOSE
TURTLE	POND	TOUGH HOPE

CROSSWORD *Hatchet*

CROSSWORD CLUES *Hatchet*

ACROSS
4 The ___ was that Brian saw his mother with another man
6 Friend that Brian created
7 They helped Brian think of ways to survive
9 The plane that rescued Brian had these
10 Brian used a ___ and arrows to kill the rabbits
11 It drove Brian to hunt
12 Plane crashed into it
14 The ___ plane didn't see Brian and turned away
18 Number of days Brian spent in the wilderness
21 Teacher who told students to value themselves
22 Mall where Brian saw his mother and the other man
24 That Brian knew he could learn and survive was ___ Hope
25 Pretended to be lost in the woods with Brian
28 The senseless attack of this animal drove Brian into the water
29 Raft Brian built to get to the plane: ___ One
31 First Meat
32 Model of the plane that crashed

DOWN
1 Where Brian stored his food after the skunk got the eggs
2 Teenage wilderness survivor
3 Brian's age
4 Brian got the ___ pack from the back of the plane
5 Brian's first food
6 The ___ buyer rescued Brian
7 What Brian's parents had gotten
8 It destroyed Brian's shelter
13 Gift from Brian's mother
15 Mr. ___ worked in the oil fields in Canada
16 Plane started out in New ___
17 Brian unknowingly activated the emergency one
19 Number of hours Brian was blinded by the skunk
20 Brian's second food
21 Author
23 Interested in Brian for a few months upon his return
24 Brian took its eggs for food
26 Brian built one to store the fresh fish
27 Where Brian was going
29 It saw Brian neat the berry bushes but did not attack
30 He died of a heart attack

CROSSWORD ANSWER KEY *Hatchet*

MACTHING QUIZ/WORKSHEET 1 - HATCHET

___ 1. POND   A. Brian built one to store the fresh fish
___ 2. FIRE   B. It drove Brian to hunt
___ 3. BRUSHPILE   C. Brian took its eggs for food
___ 4. CESSNA   D. Brian got the ___ pack from the back of the plane
___ 5. TORNADO   E. Author
___ 6. TURTLE   F. It saw Brian near the berry bushes but did not attack
___ 7. DIVORCE   G. Number of days Brian spent in the wilderness
___ 8. MOOSE   H. What Brian's parents had gotten
___ 9. FLOATS   I. The senseless attack of this animal drove Brian into the water
___10. YORK   J. He died of a heart attack
___11. SURVIVAL   K. Plane started out in New ___
___12. MOSQUITOES   L. The ___ plane didn't see Brian and turned away
___13. PILOT   M. Model of the plane that crashed
___14. BEAR   N. They made a living coat on Brian's skin
___15. PERPICH   O. Friend that Brian created
___16. ROBESON   P. Gift from Brian's mother
___17. FIFTYFOUR   Q. The ___ buyer rescued Brian
___18. SEARCH   R. It destroyed Brian's shelter
___19. HUNGER   S. Brian's age
___20. PORCUPINE   T. The plane that rescued Brian had these
___21. LEDGE   U. Teacher who told students to value themselves
___22. FUR   V. Attack of this animal caused Brian to create fire
___23. THIRTEEN   W. Raft Brian built to get to the plane: ___ One
___24. HATCHET   X. Mr. ___ worked in the oil fields in Canada
___25. PAULSEN   Y. Where Brian stored his food after the skunk got the eggs

KEY: MACTHING QUIZ/WORKSHEET 1 - HATCHET

A - 1. POND		A. Brian built one to store the fresh fish
O - 2. FIRE		B. It drove Brian to hunt
W - 3. BRUSHPILE		C. Brian took its eggs for food
M - 4. CESSNA		D. Brian got the ___ pack from the back of the plane
R - 5. TORNADO		E. Author
C - 6. TURTLE		F. It saw Brian near the berry bushes but did not attack
H - 7. DIVORCE		G. Number of days Brian spent in the wilderness
I - 8. MOOSE		H. What Brian's parents had gotten
T - 9. FLOATS		I. The senseless attack of this animal drove Brian into the water
K - 10. YORK		J. He died of a heart attack
D - 11. SURVIVAL		K. Plane started out in New ___
N - 12. MOSQUITOES		L. The ___ plane didn't see Brian and turned away
J - 13. PILOT		M. Model of the plane that crashed
F - 14. BEAR		N. They made a living coat on Brian's skin
U - 15. PERPICH		O. Friend that Brian created
X - 16. ROBESON		P. Gift from Brian's mother
G - 17. FIFTYFOUR		Q. The ___ buyer rescued Brian
L - 18. SEARCH		R. It destroyed Brian's shelter
B - 19. HUNGER		S. Brian's age
V - 20. PORCUPINE		T. The plane that rescued Brian had these
Y - 21. LEDGE		U. Teacher who told students to value themselves
Q - 22. FUR		V. Attack of this animal caused Brian to create fire
S - 23. THIRTEEN		W. Raft Brian built to get to the plane: ___ One
P - 24. HATCHET		X. Mr. ___ worked in the oil fields in Canada
E - 25. PAULSEN		Y. Where Brian stored his food after the skunk got the eggs

MACTHING QUIZ/WORKSHEET 2 - HATCHET

___ 1. FIFTYFOUR   A. What Brian's parents had gotten

___ 2. SECRET   B. Interested in Brian for a few months upon his return

___ 3. CHERRIES   C. Model of the plane that crashed

___ 4. FIRE   D. Author

___ 5. CESSNA   E. Attack of this animal caused Brian to create fire

___ 6. POND   F. That Brian knew he could learn and survive was ___ Hope

___ 7. PORCUPINE   G. Brian's first food

___ 8. DIVORCE   H. Number of days Brian spent in the wilderness

___ 9. PRESS   I. The ___ plane didn't see Brian and turned away

___ 10. BRIAN   J. The plane that rescued Brian had these

___ 11. SEARCH   K. Pretended to be lost in the woods with Brian

___ 12. DREAMS   L. It drove Brian to hunt

___ 13. YORK   M. Teenage wilderness survivor

___ 14. FLOATS   N. Raft Brian built to get to the plane: ___ One

___ 15. BOW   O. Brian's age

___ 16. HUNGER   P. Friend that Brian created

___ 17. THIRTEEN   Q. Brian's second food

___ 18. TURTLE   R. They helped Brian think of ways to survive

___ 19. RASPBERRIES   S. The ___ was that Brian saw his mother with another man

___ 20. BRUSHPILE   T. Brian built one to store the fresh fish

___ 21. PAULSEN   U. Plane started out in New ___

___ 22. TOUGH   V. Brian took its eggs for food

___ 23. TERRY   W. He died of a heart attack

___ 24. PILOT   X. The ___ buyer rescued Brian

___ 25. FUR   Y. Brian used a ___ and arrows to kill the rabbits

KEY: MACTHING QUIZ/WORKSHEET 2 - HATCHET

H - 1.	FIFTYFOUR	A. What Brian's parents had gotten
S - 2.	SECRET	B. Interested in Brian for a few months upon his return
G - 3.	CHERRIES	C. Model of the plane that crashed
P - 4.	FIRE	D. Author
C - 5.	CESSNA	E. Attack of this animal caused Brian to create fire
T - 6.	POND	F. That Brian knew he could learn and survive was ___ Hope
E - 7.	PORCUPINE	G. Brian's first food
A - 8.	DIVORCE	H. Number of days Brian spent in the wilderness
B - 9.	PRESS	I. The ___ plane didn't see Brian and turned away
M - 10.	BRIAN	J. The plane that rescued Brian had these
I - 11.	SEARCH	K. Pretended to be lost in the woods with Brian
R - 12.	DREAMS	L. It drove Brian to hunt
U - 13.	YORK	M. Teenage wilderness survivor
J - 14.	FLOATS	N. Raft Brian built to get to the plane: ___ One
Y - 15.	BOW	O. Brian's age
L - 16.	HUNGER	P. Friend that Brian created
O - 17.	THIRTEEN	Q. Brian's second food
V - 18.	TURTLE	R. They helped Brian think of ways to survive
Q - 19.	RASPBERRIES	S. The ___ was that Brian saw his mother with another man
N - 20.	BRUSHPILE	T. Brian built one to store the fresh fish
D - 21.	PAULSEN	U. Plane started out in New ___
F - 22.	TOUGH	V. Brian took its eggs for food
K - 23.	TERRY	W. He died of a heart attack
W - 24.	PILOT	X. The ___ buyer rescued Brian
X - 25.	FUR	Y. Brian used a ___ and arrows to kill the rabbits

JUGGLE LETTER REVIEW GAME CLUE SHEET - HATCHET

1. BIODLOFR = 1. _____
First Meat

2. URTTLE = 2. _____
Brian took its eggs for food

3. UNELSAP = 3. _____
Author

4. ERAPRBRSISE = 4. _____
Brian's second food

5. ROIUYTFFF = 5. _____
Number of days Brian spent in the wilderness

6. DONATRO = 6. _____
It destroyed Brian's shelter

7. CIVEODR = 7. _____
What Brian's parents had gotten

8. BOW = 8. _____
Brian used a ___ and arrows to kill the rabbits

9. RTYER = 9. _____
Pretended to be lost in the woods with Brian

10. OPDN =10. _____
Brian built one to store the fresh fish

11. PLHBURESI =11. _____
Raft Brian built to get to the plane: ___ One

12. SRSEP =12. _____
Interested in Brian for a few months upon his return

13. EMSOO =13. _____
The senseless attack of this animal drove Brian into the water

14. KROY =14. _____
Plane started out in New ___

15. RHTTNEEI =15. _____
Brian's age

16. TOOQIMSESU =16. _____
They made a living coat on Brian's skin

17. IFRE =17. _____
Friend that Brian created

18. TAECTHH =18. _____
Gift from Brian's mother

19. EAMRB =19. _____
Mall where Brian saw his mother and the other man

20. OEORBSN =20. _____
Mr. ___ worked in the oil fields in Canada

21. REAB =21. _____
It saw Brian near the berry bushes but did not attack

22. PHIECPR =22. _____
Teacher who told students to value themselves

23. EGNUHR =23. _____
It drove Brian to hunt

24. ETCERS =24. _____
The ___ was that Brian saw his mother with another man

25. MARDSE =25. _____
They helped Brian think of ways to survive

KEY: JUGGLE LETTER REVIEW GAME CLUE SHEET - HATCHET

1. BIODLOFR = 1. FOOLBIRD
   First Meat

2. URTTLE = 2. TURTLE
   Brian took its eggs for food

3. UNELSAP = 3. PAULSEN
   Author

4. ERAPRBRSISE = 4. RASPBERRIES
   Brian's second food

5. ROIUYTFFF = 5. FIFTYFOUR
   Number of days Brian spent in the wilderness

6. DONATRO = 6. TORNADO
   It destroyed Brian's shelter

7. CIVEODR = 7. DIVORCE
   What Brian's parents had gotten

8. BOW = 8. BOW
   Brian used a ___ and arrows to kill the rabbits

9. RTYER = 9. TERRY
   Pretended to be lost in the woods with Brian

10. OPDN =10. POND
    Brian built one to store the fresh fish

11. PLHBURESI =11. BRUSHPILE
    Raft Brian built to get to the plane: ___ One

12. SRSEP =12. PRESS
    Interested in Brian for a few months upon his return

13. EMSOO =13. MOOSE
    The senseless attack of this animal drove Brian into the water

14. KROY =14. YORK
Plane started out in New ___

15. RHTTNEEI =15. THIRTEEN
Brian's age

16. TOOQIMSESU =16. MOSQUITOES
They made a living coat on Brian's skin

17. IFRE =17. FIRE
Friend that Brian created

18. TAECTHH =18. HATCHET
Gift from Brian's mother

19. EAMRB =19. AMBER
Mall where Brian saw his mother and the other man

20. OEORBSN =20. ROBESON
Mr. ___ worked in the oil fields in Canada

21. REAB =21. BEAR
It saw Brian near the berry bushes but did not attack

22. PHIECPR =22. PERPICH
Teacher who told students to value themselves

23. EGNUHR =23. HUNGER
It drove Brian to hunt

24. ETCERS =24. SECRET
The ___ was that Brian saw his mother with another man

25. MARDSE =25. DREAMS
They helped Brian think of ways to survive

VOCABULARY RESOURCES

VOCABULARY WORD SEARCH *Hatchet*

All the words in this list are associated with *Hatchet* with emphasis on the vocabulary words. The words are placed backwards, forward, diagonally, up and down.

```
E R S M A C X L M G T I R G
X F U S X R E M N A G O R S
A Q A A I U L I P D S E L T
S B G P T D P I N G X I G A
P M A S S E T D L O R I N B
E E A T E R E E M D O F I L
R N L S E G G D N R M Y T E
A T S P E D V E W O L L A W
T O L R R E T C L O S U I O
I M D O O T H E F T E D R U
O X N N G L D R S G V O U L
N E P G F U R O R G E S F H
B L E R A X E O G O D A N L
I S S O D E G N U L L T I N
```

ABATED	ASSET	CRUDE
DRONE	EXASPERATION	EXULTED
FUROR	GORGE	HEFTED
INFURIATING	LUNGED	PRONG
RECEDED	SEEPING	SPASM
STABLE	TENDRILS	WALLOW

VOCABULARY CROSSWORD *Hatchet*

VOCABULARY CROSSWORD CLUES *Hatchet*

ACROSS
1 Steady; firm
4 Stuff; devour
6 Thin, pointed, projecting point
7 Rough
10 Valuable
11 Withdrew; went back
13 Disinfectant; kills germs
15 Tearing; turning; twisting
17 A continuous humming sound
18 Waving or swinging vigorously
21 Stumped; stuck in puzzlement
24 Rejoiced
25 Enduring; not giving up
27 Excessively
28 Twisting; winding

DOWN
2 Long, slender, curling strands
3 Intense excitement
5 Twisting the face to show pain
8 Lifted; heaved
9 Piercing; intense
12 Section; part
13 Advantage; resource
14 Aggravating; maddening
16 Roll around
19 Dashed; charged
20 Lessened; diminished
21 Dripping; trickling
22 Enormously
23 Regretfully
26 Involuntary muscle contraction

VOCABULARY CROSSWORD ANSWER KEY *Hatchet*

Across: STABLE, GORGE, PRONG, CRUDE, PRECIOUS, RECEDED, ANTISEPTIC, WRENCHING, DRONE, FLAILING, STYMIED, EXULTED, PERSISTENT, UNDULY, SPIRALING

Down: SEDATE, FROG, ERROR, GRIMACE, HRDFLESS, RUDDER, KEEL, PROFUSELY, CARCASS, ASSESSMENT, RINGING, SWAYING, UNWIELDY, FURIOUSLY, ALLURING, PLAGUES, TRIGGERED, BRAGGART, INGRATE, WEDGED, UNDEFEATED, SLEEPING, PIVES, PASM, LY, LILY

VOCABULARY WORKSEET 1 - HATCHET

___ 1. ASSET   A. Stumped; stuck in puzzlement
___ 2. RECEDED   B. Roll around
___ 3. PRECIOUS   C. Rough
___ 4. SEGMENT   D. Long, slender, curling strands
___ 5. HEFTED   E. Piercing; intense
___ 6. WALLOW   F. Section; part
___ 7. EXASPERATION   G. Valuable
___ 8. FUROR   H. Twisting; winding
___ 9. FLAILING   I. Annoyance
___ 10. WRENCHING   J. Tearing; turning; twisting
___ 11. STAGGERING   K. Stuff; devour
___ 12. RUEFULLY   L. Waving or swinging vigorously
___ 13. SPIRALING   M. Enormously
___ 14. KEENING   N. Dashed; charged
___ 15. STABLE   O. Advantage; resource
___ 16. PERSISTENT   P. Thin, pointed, projecting part
___ 17. STYMIED   Q. Intense excitement
___ 18. MASSIVELY   R. Lifted; heaved
___ 19. LUNGED   S. Twisting the face to show pain
___ 20. CRUDE   T. Enduring; not giving up
___ 21. PRONG   U. Withdrew; went back
___ 22. ABATED   V. Overwhelming
___ 23. GORGE   W. Steady; firm
___ 24. TENDRILS   X. Lessened; diminished
___ 25. GRIMACING   Y. Regretfully

KEY: VOCABULARY WORKSEET 1 - HATCHET

O - 1. ASSET		A. Stumped; stuck in puzzlement
U - 2. RECEDED		B. Roll around
G - 3. PRECIOUS		C. Rough
F - 4. SEGMENT		D. Long, slender, curling strands
R - 5. HEFTED		E. Piercing; intense
B - 6. WALLOW		F. Section; part
I - 7. EXASPERATION		G. Valuable
Q - 8. FUROR		H. Twisting; winding
L - 9. FLAILING		I. Annoyance
J - 10. WRENCHING		J. Tearing; turning; twisting
V - 11. STAGGERING		K. Stuff; devour
Y - 12. RUEFULLY		L. Waving or swinging vigorously
H - 13. SPIRALING		M. Enormously
E - 14. KEENING		N. Dashed; charged
W 15. STABLE		O. Advantage; resource
T - 16. PERSISTENT		P. Thin, pointed, projecting part
A - 17. STYMIED		Q. Intense excitement
M - 18. MASSIVELY		R. Lifted; heaved
N - 19. LUNGED		S. Twisting the face to show pain
C - 20. CRUDE		T. Enduring; not giving up
P - 21. PRONG		U. Withdrew; went back
X - 22. ABATED		V. Overwhelming
K - 23. GORGE		W. Steady; firm
D - 24. TENDRILS		X. Lessened; diminished
S - 25. GRIMACING		Y. Regretfully

VOCABULARY WORKSEET 2 - HATCHET

___ 1. WALLOW   A. Lifted; heaved
___ 2. ABATED   B. Enduring; not giving up
___ 3. STYMIED   C. Involuntary muscle contraction
___ 4. ASSET   D. Intense excitement
___ 5. HEFTED   E. Dashed; charged
___ 6. GORGE   F. Dripping; trickling
___ 7. PERSISTENT   G. Waving or swinging vigorously
___ 8. CRUDE   H. An electronic devise that sends a signal
___ 9. LUNGED   I. Lessened; diminished
___10. RECEDED   J. Natural; intuitive
___11. STABLE   K. Stumped; stuck in puzzlement
___12. GRIMACING   L. Piercing; intense
___13. EXULTED   M. Rejoiced
___14. PRECIOUS   N. Valuable
___15. DRONE   O. A continuous humming sound
___16. UNDULY   P. Excessively
___17. FLAILING   Q. Roll around
___18. SPASM   R. Advantage; resource
___19. TRANSMITTER   S. Steady; firm
___20. EXASPERATION   T. Twisting the face to show pain
___21. FUROR   U. Withdrew; went back
___22. INSTINCTIVE   V. Aggravating; maddening
___23. KEENING   W. Stuff; devour
___24. SEEPING   X. Rough
___25. INFURIATING   Y. Annoyance

KEY: VOCABULARY WORKSEET 2 - HATCHET

Q - 1.	WALLOW	A. Lifted; heaved
I - 2.	ABATED	B. Enduring; not giving up
K - 3.	STYMIED	C. Involuntary muscle contraction
R - 4.	ASSET	D. Intense excitement
A - 5.	HEFTED	E. Dashed; charged
W 6.	GORGE	F. Dripping; trickling
B - 7.	PERSISTENT	G. Waving or swinging vigorously
X - 8.	CRUDE	H. An electronic devise that sends a signal
E - 9.	LUNGED	I. Lessened; diminished
U -10.	RECEDED	J. Natural; intuitive
S -11.	STABLE	K. Stumped; stuck in puzzlement
T -12.	GRIMACING	L. Piercing; intense
M -13.	EXULTED	M. Rejoiced
N -14.	PRECIOUS	N. Valuable
O -15.	DRONE	O. A continuous humming sound
P -16.	UNDULY	P. Excessively
G -17.	FLAILING	Q. Roll around
C -18.	SPASM	R. Advantage; resource
H -19.	TRANSMITTER	S. Steady; firm
Y -20.	EXASPERATION	T. Twisting the face to show pain
D -21.	FUROR	U. Withdrew; went back
J - 22.	INSTINCTIVE	V. Aggravating; maddening
L -23.	KEENING	W. Stuff; devour
F -24.	SEEPING	X. Rough
V -25.	INFURIATING	Y. Annoyance

VOCABULARY JUGGLE LETTER REVIEW GAME CLUES - HATCHET

1. NETEGMS = 1. _____
   Section; part

2. REGGO = 2. _____
   Stuff; devour

3. ESTABL = 3. _____
   Steady; firm

4. NHICRENWG = 4. _____
   Tearing; turning; twisting

5. TPANSTECII = 5. _____
   Disinfectant; kills germs

6. UNDELG = 6. _____
   Dashed; charged

7. EONDR = 7. _____
   A continuous humming sound

8. NESPGIE = 8. _____
   Dripping; trickling

9. LIIFALNG = 9. _____
   Waving or swinging vigorously

10. RTAESRNTMTI =10. _____
    An electronic devise that sends a signal

11. OSCIPERU =11. _____
    Valuable

12. DELNTISR =12. _____
    Long, slender, curling strands

13. OLLAWW =13. _____
    Roll around

14. UCEYTLRCAA =14. _____
                    Correctly

15. RNGOP   =15. _____
                    Thin, pointed, projecting part

16. DUERC   =16. _____
                    Rough

17. IUNFITNGAIR =17. _____
                    Aggravating; maddening

18. SEATS   =18. _____
                    Advantage; resource

19. EKGENNI   =19. _____
                    Piercing; intense

20. ULFYLUER   =20. _____
                    Regretfully

21. ISGTNAGRGE =21. _____
                    Overwhelming

22. ANMCGIGRI   =22. _____
                    Twisting the face to show pain

23. IDRUELEVZP =23. _____
                    Ground up; crumbled

24. EIYMDST   =24. _____
                    Stumped; stuck in puzzlement

25. IPIRGNLAS   =25. _____
                    Twisting; winding

KEY: VOCABULARY JUGGLE LETTER REVIEW GAME CLUES - HATCHET

1. NETEGMS = 1. SEGMENT
Section; part

2. REGGO = 2. GORGE
Stuff; devour

3. ESTABL = 3. STABLE
Steady; firm

4. NHICRENWG = 4. WRENCHING
Tearing; turning; twisting

5. TPANSTECII = 5. ANTISEPTIC
Disinfectant; kills germs

6. UNDELG = 6. LUNGED
Dashed; charged

7. EONDR = 7. DRONE
A continuous humming sound

8. NESPGIE = 8. SEEPING
Dripping; trickling

9. LIIFALNG = 9. FLAILING
Waving or swinging vigorously

10. RTAESRNTMTI =10. TRANSMITTER
An electronic devise that sends a signal

11. OSCIPERU =11. PRECIOUS
Valuable

12. DELNTISR =12. TENDRILS
Long, slender, curling strands

13. OLLAWW =13. WALLOW
Roll around

14. UCEYTLRCAA =14. ACCURATELY
Correctly

15. RNGOP =15. PRONG
Thin, pointed, projecting part

16. DUERC =16. CRUDE
Rough

17. IUNFITNGAIR =17. INFURIATING
Aggravating; maddening

18. SEATS =18. ASSET
Advantage; resource

19. EKGENNI =19. KEENING
Piercing; intense

20. ULFYLUER =20. RUEFULLY
Regretfully

21. ISGTNAGRGE =21. STAGGERING
Overwhelming

22. ANMCGIGRI =22. GRIMACING
Twisting the face to show pain

23. IDRUELEVZP =23. PULVERIZED
Ground up; crumbled

24. EIYMDST =24. STYMIED
Stumped; stuck in puzzlement

25. IPIRGNLAS =25. SPIRALING
Twisting; winding

www.ingramcontent.com/pod-product-compliance
Lightning Source LLC
Chambersburg PA
CBHW051411070526
44584CB00023B/3386